IN SEARCH
OF HUMANITY

IN SEARCH OF HUMANITY

WHY WE FIGHT, HOW TO STOP, AND THE ROLE BUSINESS MUST PLAY

JARIK CONRAD, EdD

In Search of Humanity

Why We Fight, How to Stop, and the Role Business Must Play

ISBN 978-1-5445-3012-3 Hardcover

      978-1-5445-3013-0 Paperback

      978-1-5445-3014-7 Ebook

Alexandria and Jarik,

I wrote this book for you.

I want you to come of age in a world
where human diversity is valued and recognized
as a source of strength rather than a subject
of controversy and conflict.

CONTENTS

PART 2
DIVERSITY, EQUITY, INCLUSION, AND BELONGING

INTRODUCTION

In Search of an Identity

To the rest of the world, America must look like it has dissociative identity disorder, its split personalities continually struggling for primacy. At times, we are the moral conscience of the world, pushing other countries to prioritize human rights and embrace environmental responsibility. Sometimes, we are a rich and powerful bully that uses brute force to bend others to our will. At other times, we are a fragile democracy fighting to retain a position of strength, stability, and influence.

America has been cleaved in two, with little in the way of constructive solutions. We are in the throes of a perennial civil war, pitting traditionalists against reformists. While this conflict has endured since the birth of the nation, with battles won and lost by each side, something feels different about the present period. The tense political and social divides are pitting coworkers, neighbors, and family members against each other, sometimes resulting in violence. Humans can be incredibly kind, but our evolutionally wiring also enables us to be astonishingly cruel.

There are two clear options for America to bring a firm conclusion to its civil war—find a common enemy to gang up on, or unite around a common goal. I vote for the second option. Let's harness the energy and emotion on both sides and redirect it to galvanize people around a clear and compelling rallying cry, one that is uniquely American.

What could this clarion call be? America's most sacred symbols may hold the key. The Declaration of Independence is inscribed, "We hold these truths to be self-evident, that all men are created equal, that they are endowed by their Creator with certain unalienable Rights, that among these are Life, Liberty and the pursuit of Happiness." The word "liberty," or the concept of freedom, has a prominent place in the text. This is ironic because the text was written during the lifetime enslavement of Black people. How can all people be created equal if the children of Black people are born into bondage? The Pledge of Allegiance, recited in classrooms all over America, ends with "one nation, indivisible, with liberty and justice for all." The national anthem ends with "the land of the free and the home of the brave." Then, there is the Statue of Liberty, originally proposed as a symbol of freedom to commemorate the abolishment of slavery.

These symbols of yesteryear advanced the idea of unity and freedom as the distinguishing characteristics of America. Yet these characteristics are at the heart of America's civil war today. Traditionalists interpret freedom as autonomy and independence—no government intrusion in their personal lives. Reformists interpret freedom as fairness and egalitarianism—equal rights and opportunities. Obviously, there are stark differences of opinion.

The reformists' interpretation of freedom hardly exists in America. Individuals who are born poor are significantly more likely to remain poor, and individuals born wealthy are significantly more likely to remain wealthy. As long as Black people (and poor White people) continue to be treated as inferior human beings, taxpayer-funded government social programs will continue to be needed. None of us will be free until all of us are free.

It's time for a new Reconstruction, one that overcomes the shortfalls and failures of past Reconstruction eras. To have any legitimate hope of achieving the freedom exalted in our most sacred symbols and ceremonies, we must finally make good on the promise the nation made to its Black citizens during the first Reconstruction that began in 1865 and ended in 1877—comparable economic footing and political influence as enjoyed by White people.

As of this writing, America itself hangs in the balance—the summer of 2020 saw thousands of individuals from all backgrounds protest against structural and systemic racism in the aftermath of the police killings of George Floyd, Breonna Taylor, and so many other unarmed Black people. In 2021, a violent insurrection at the US Capitol, carried out by a hodgepodge of individuals and groups, including White supremacists, was determined to stop the certification of a lawful presidential election. On top of that, the increasingly bold nature of racist and hateful comments and behaviors is giving

Black people a glimpse of what life must have been like for their grandparents.

When Americans treat other Americans badly, we must resist the urge to say, "This is not who we are," because truthfully, it is *absolutely who we are.* Instead, let's work together across ideological and demographic lines to build a new "America," one that acknowledges and rectifies past transgressions and commits everlastingly to diversity, equity, inclusion, and belonging. True patriotism is the extent to which we treat each other with abiding dignity and respect. We can find common ground, but it requires a willingness to relinquish the perspective that one group of people has a superior claim to all that is good in life.

All human beings are, in fact, created equal. Once born, however, inequality surfaces. I learned this as a child in East St. Louis, Illinois, growing up in public housing. Looking today at photos of the home to which we later moved and its garage patched together with found pieces of wood, the term "war zone" springs to mind. It felt like that too, with a crime rate that frequently made East St. Louis one of the most dangerous cities in America. In 1991, the year after I graduated from high school, the *St. Louis Post-Dispatch* called my hometown the "most distressed small city" in the country. Three-quarters of the population lived on welfare.

In my high school, the science lab had no equipment, the classrooms had limited supplies, and the restrooms had few working toilets. None of my schools had football fields, swimming pools, baseball diamonds, or soccer fields. I find it amusing that people who complain about "throwing money at problems" rarely suffer from a lack of resources themselves. Despite the city's challenges, I met some of the smartest and kindest people in East St. Louis, a place that has produced people with remarkable talents, including jazz giant Miles Davis, Olympic superstar Jackie Joyner-Kersee, and former US ambassador and permanent representative to the United Nations Donald McHenry.

Although conditions were certainly demoralizing, I never felt inferior as a young child, unlike some of my peers. I hated watching television reports suggesting that the outside world thought of me as such. In retrospect, I developed a belief that my family was somehow better off and more deserving of success, even though my mother was a single parent living on welfare. Even though we did not go on vacations, even though I never owned a pair of Air Jordans, and even though we never went to restaurants and almost always ate cheap, processed foods high in sugar, salt, and fat, I somehow felt we were different. I refused to give up on my future. I simply would not accept settling for less because I was Black and born in the ghetto. I know I am outlier who represents what is possible but not probable. Many others I knew in East St. Louis never escaped the invisible chains that weighed down their hopes. My heart is with them and the countless others born into neglected communities across America.

This story must change. Once the country allows Black people to cash in on the promissory note that Dr. Martin Luther King Jr. indicated had been stamped "insufficient funds," we can all stand as proud Americans, our flag a true symbol of encompassing liberty and justice. Diversity, equity, inclusion, and belonging can become our differentiating source of strength as a nation. Otherwise, this ominous civil war will fester for generations to come.

In this book, expect to read a history of numbing social and economic inequality, of government promises made but not kept, and of ineffective plans put forth to level the field by politicians whose policies are paid for by powerful industry interests. Expect also to read why the American Dream is a fantasy designed to enrich a few people, and how this country came to be what it has become over history. Most importantly, expect to read how change can be achieved against such overwhelming odds. No longer must we trust solely in our governing bodies to drive change. American companies, many of them complicit in maintaining inequality as the status quo, must partner with *our* government to create a new America.

PART 1

TO THE
VICTOR GO
THE SPOILS

CHAPTER 1

HUMANITY AT A CROSSROADS

The impulse that inspired early human beings to adapt and explore new habitats is the same basic instinct driving people and all other species in the animal kingdom today—the unrelenting desire to survive. Guiding us in this quest is our curiosity.

People are enamored with understanding the "why?" and "why not?" of things. Keenly observing our surroundings and making connections between cause and effect have been critical to our survival. Children grow and mature by understanding the relationship between an event or condition and the results that emanate from them, which promotes learning and increases the odds of survival.

The importance of curiosity as a survival mechanism is evident in brain scans. The brain releases dopamine as a reward and as a reinforcement when we engage in behaviors that increase our likelihood of survival.

Two types of human curiosity are visible in functional MRI brain scans—perceptual curiosity and epistemic curiosity.

Perceptual curiosity involves solving immediate needs, such as exploring the refrigerator to determine what to eat for lunch. Epistemic curiosity, on the other hand, is concerned with bigger questions, such as, "How far away are the stars in the sky?" Both forms of curiosity are necessary, deeply satisfying, and beneficial for the whole of society.

Thanks to the unwavering curiosity we inherited from our ancestors, we live in a remarkable era of human development. Across the centuries, scientists have answered many of humanity's most enduring and perplexing questions. Engineers have developed machines that make things and afford travel worldwide. Athletes have achieved feats never thought humanly possible. Companies are using digital technologies like advanced analytics to predict business outcomes and automated machines to make defect-free products at scale. Not only have astronauts walked on the moon, but Captain Kirk himself, ninety-year-old William Shatner, has flown to space on a ship built by billionaire businessman Jeff Bezos. Pharmaceutical giants, in partnership with biopharma firms, have made vaccines and therapies at warp speed in the battle against the COVID-19 pandemic, which as of this writing was in an uncertain retreat thanks to successful vaccinations of hundreds of millions of people worldwide.

Much more is in store, all of it driven by human curiosity and our basic need to survive. Scientists are poised to cure insidious chronic illnesses, such as cancer and Alzheimer's disease. Harmful emissions will decrease substantially as fully electric cars, planes, and even locomotives become the norm. Thanks to technology, work will become more collaborative, efficient, and flexible insofar as where, when, and how people work. For people in the developed world, smart homes and personal devices will provide an unprecedented level of convenience.

This "promised land" is strewn with potholes, however. If human curiosity yields benefits aimed solely at the wealthy, social divisions will widen. Governments and businesses spend capital on inventions and enterprises that serve objectives of trivial value to humanity at large. SpaceX founder Elon Musk, for instance, is planning to one-up Bezos by establishing communities of people on Mars. He has made several successful launches in this regard, traveling onboard himself in 2021 to the edge of space, when so many individuals have unsatisfying lives here on Earth. Companies develop automation technologies to enhance labor efficiencies but give scant consideration to the reduced employment levels that ensue.

More than 25 percent of jobs in the US have experienced high levels of disruption due to automation, and 37 percent of workers are worried about losing their jobs because of it. By 2022, the total task hours completed by humans will drop by 13 percent, and by 2030, robots may displace an astonishing 20 million manufacturing jobs. The prospect of losing their job has impelled seven in ten people to consider using treatments to enhance their brain and body if it will improve their employment opportunities in the future.

Another adverse outcome is our reliance on technology dampening our curiosity—the mechanism helping humanity problem-solve and think critically for millennia. Speed and convenience generally top the list of consumer preferences for products we use daily. But smart devices manage us as opposed to the other way around, impelling us toward a future where we may not need to get out of bed to do much of anything. Robot assistants will handle our needs—for those of us who can afford them.

What is the consequence of this uber-convenience on our curiosity? As John Aberman writes in his *Washington Post* article chronicling his interview with Mario Livio, author of *Why? What Makes Us Curious*, "Without a framework that rewards and encourages curiosity, we will lose the very trait that is essential to our future."

Three other essential traits born of our survival instincts—tribalism, violent behavior, and fear—enabled us to push rival hominids into extinction but now threaten the existence of our species. These traits, alone or working together, have resulted in such inhuman crimes and conditions as sex trafficking, sexual assault, violence, hunger, homelessness, and chronic illness, affecting Black, Brown, and poor families at greater numbers than the population at large.

COVID-19 is just the latest reminder of the disparate demographic experiences infecting and killing such populations at much higher rates than White and/or wealthy individuals. The coronavirus has devastated the poorest populations in the world's richest countries. For such people, COVID-19 is a pandemic within a protracted and incessant health crisis, exacerbating their existing struggles.

The reason this can happen in the so-called developed world is the predatory instinct we inherited from our ancestors, which was as important to our survival in the harsh competitive environment of the early African savanna as our curiosity. We have not tamed our predatory ways, whether it is hunting other species for sport or exploiting less fortunate humans. Meanwhile, the gap between the "haves" and the "have nots" continues to widen. One of my former business school professors, Dr. Robert Frank, wrote in *Winner-Take-All-Society: Why the Few at the Top Get So Much More Than the Rest of Us* that America has built institutions and an economy destined to yield ever-increasing income inequality. We have seen this play out in the K-shaped COVID-19 recovery. "Wealthy individuals and white-collar workers have been able to work from home and more seamlessly adjust to the COVID challenges, while service workers have been laid off en masse, and other front-line workers, especially first responders, have had little choice but return to work and bear the brunt of the pandemic. Simply put, "the outbreak has hit working-class communities hardest is hardly a surprise," according to economist Peter Atwater.

TRIBALISM

Regarding the origins of tribalism and why we continue to separate ourselves into groups, David Berreby, award-winning author of *Us and Them: The Science of Identity*, says, "We don't have wings. We don't have claws. We don't have really big teeth, and we have no ability to change colors like an octopus. If you picture us as animals competing in the African savannah, we're just not equipped to deal with a lion. This isn't unique to us. Most primate species are stuck with the same problem. What do we do instead without the physical survival tools other animals have? We live in groups, and the group is extremely important to keeping us alive in many ways."

From Berreby's perspective, being an independent thinker on the African savanna is a ticket to one's death. If a tiger is chasing you, the path of escape is not nearly as important as how many people take this path with you. Tribalism also fostered the transmission of knowledge needed for survival. People learned from other people what was safe and what was not. If someone ate a mushroom and died, it was a clear signal not to eat that type of mushroom. This information was retained and passed down through generations.

We still rely on this pack mentality to keep us physically and emotionally safe. Studies indicate the single biggest factor contributing to happiness in life is the quality of relationships. We are social creatures. We need each other. Yet when we group together into the equivalent of a tribe today, we tend to do it with people who live as we do and share similar experiences and perspectives about the world. Our relative sameness provides feelings of security and confidence.

The best indication of sameness is how someone looks. At birth, babies are wired to seek out the faces of people who resemble their caretakers. Conversely, people who look different are perceived as a threat. From an evolutionary standpoint, this makes sense, as the inability to immediately recognize a friend or foe meant the difference between life and death.

That early training stays with us. As adults meeting someone for the first time today, visual clues such as a person's race—the distinctive physical characteristics shared by a category of humankind—are unconsciously analyzed. The brain does a split-second calculation to determine the probability that another person will be safe, or "one of ours."

Other cues suggesting likeness can foster ingrained biases and discriminatory practices. For example, when people exhibit different cultural norms or hold opposing viewpoints, it may cause us to question our own beliefs and lifestyle practices. This circumspection is uncomfortable and unsafe for many people. As a result, we may lash out at other groups.

Examples of this behavior abound, including the rise in nationalism reshaping global geopolitics and the mass migrations of desperate refugees fleeing their home countries to perceived "safe" havens in nations that nonetheless greet them as invaders. Racism and other social ills like sexism, homophobia, and xenophobia have driven a wedge between people across the world. If you happen to be in the wrong tribe, your life does not matter as much as the lives of fellow human beings in other tribes.

VIOLENCE

Many people who watched the video of the murder of George Floyd by the police on the streets of Minneapolis were horrified by the abject cruelty displayed. Yet it was not all that long ago in the annals of humankind when Americans dressed up in their Sunday best to watch disobedient slaves hanged in Southern town squares. Even after slavery was abolished, this perverse form of entertainment—lynching—continued in the South. Between 1877 and 1950, nearly 4,000 Black men, women, and children were lynched. The 1916 racially motivated hanging of Jesse Washington, watched by some 10,000 people and preserved in horrific photographs, is a palpable reminder of the suffering endured by Black people. A moving memorial to slaves who were lynched has been erected at the Legacy Museum, which has been built on the site of a former warehouse where enslaved Black people were imprisoned in Montgomery, Alabama.

A Cruel and Brutal Practice

A picture postcard depicts a crowd of spectators at the lynching of Jesse Washington in Waco, Texas, 1916. *(Photo from Library of Congress.)*

Jesse Washington was a seventeen-year-old mentally disabled Black farmhand who was lynched in Waco, Texas, on May 15, 1916. Washington was convicted of raping the wife of his White employer. After a four-minute deliberation that found him guilty, Washington was taken down the back stairs of the courthouse and attacked by an angry White mob. Spectators placed a chain around his neck and dragged him out of the county court into the street where he was paraded while being stabbed, beaten, held down, and castrated. He was then lynched in front of Waco's city hall, his body hanging in the air until it was lowered into a fiery box. In the process, his fingers and toes were amputated and sold as souvenirs. After the fire was extinguished, his charred body was dragged to Robinsonville, the scene of the murder, and left hanging from a telephone pole. These varied horrors occurred in front of an estimated 10,000 to 15,000 cheering spectators, including city officials, police, young children, and a photographer who captured the grizzly images.

These tragedies occurred because on some atavistic level, they made people feel good. Fighting and killing was a necessary aspect of early life for humans. If our ancestors were averse to combat, we, their descendants, likely would not be here. In fighting to survive, the brain rewarded both parties engaged in combat by releasing dopamine, making the violence somewhat pleasurable.

Studying the evolutionary chain of human beings, researchers confirm we have inherited a propensity for violence. Marks and scrapes on skeletons of early *Homo sapiens* document the violence they experienced in fighting to survive, individually and collectively.

The average number of in-group deaths caused by nonhuman mammals through acts of aggression, infanticide, and cannibalism was 0.3 percent, compared to a 2 percent rate of deaths through similar acts among early humans in the Paleolithic period, making us six times more likely than other mammals to kill each other.

Violent tendencies were particularly prominent among males, given the drive to eliminate competition for reproduction and necessary resources for survival. Violence among males was so prevalent, researchers theorize our ancestors invented acts of corporal punishment like caning, flogging, and branding to maintain dominance over other males.

Violence continues to be a defining aspect of human existence, evident throughout recorded history in ethnic, religious, and/or territorial disputes. Altogether, more than 300 million people have lost their lives in wars and armed conflicts, in addition to some 44 million non-combatant deaths as a result of war crimes and atrocities. And over 42 million people have succumbed to genocide, ethnic cleansing, and mass ethnic or religious persecution.

A surprising number of these atrocities happened in our lifetimes. The United States Holocaust Memorial Museum details cases of genocide occurring in Burma, Bosnia, Cambodia, the Middle East, Rwanda, Sudan, and Syria in the past half-decade. Global terrorist attacks alone have resulted in the deaths of approximately 18,643 people per year between 2016 and 2019. In the United States, more than 3 million people are victims of violent crimes annually. In 2019 alone, 417 mass shootings of people occurred, adding up to more than one shooting per day.

In 2020, as the pandemic raged and social unrest erupted in cities across America over the killings of unarmed Black people by the police, violence was on display. Fomented by White supremacists, QAnon conspiracists, and other ultra-right-wing forms of terrorism, hate crimes reached the highest level in twelve years.

"White supremacy and far-right extremism are among the greatest domestic-security threats facing the United States," US Department of Justice official Thomas T. Cullen wrote in a *New York Times* op-ed on February 22, 2019. "Regrettably, over the past twenty-five years, law enforcement, at both the Federal and State levels, has been slow to respond... Killings committed by individuals and groups associated with far-right extremist groups have risen significantly."

The violence did not abate in 2021. Following Donald Trump's meritless claims that the presidential election won by Joe Biden was stolen via an international communist conspiracy, rigged voting machines, and polling place fraud, a large mob of White people, including White supremacists, attacked the US Capitol as a joint session of Congress formally counted the electoral votes, leaving five people dead and dozens injured. Former President Trump's incitement of the insurrection resulted in his second impeachment by Congress.

We have reached a point in America where we not only accept violence as part of our daily lives but relish it, watching violent acts of aggression on social media that inevitably become viral videos. Blockbuster shoot-'em-up action movies and graphic video games depict gruesome scenes of violence in vivid detail. Many chart-topping songs promote and glorify violence. And brutal full-contact combat sports like mixed martial arts, one of the world's most watched sports today, feed the primitive human hunger for violence.

A modicum of progress has been attained. Compared to the 2 percent rate of human-versus-human deaths of early times and the much higher 12 percent murder rate of medieval times, Americans live in a relatively safe era. Rates of homicide in modern societies with police forces, legal systems, prisons, and a strong cultural attitude that rejects violence are 0.01 percent (less than 1 in 10,000 deaths).

Yet violence remains a troubling part of our lives. Humans are apex predators, meaning we have no natural predators. Compared to other apex predators like tigers, polar bears, and great white sharks, we are super apex predators. Not only do we kill more animals at alarmingly higher rates than their natural predators, we kill their natural predators too. Like other predators, we hunt for food. But unlike other predators, we also hunt for sport. We even call the animals we hunt *game*. Hunters feel a profound sense of achievement when they haul in their kill, all part of that evolutionary wiring we have maintained.

Beyond the thrill of the kill, status is a significant driver behind our predatory instinct. Hunters display evidence of their triumphs on the walls of homes. Others pay poor people to risk their lives killing exotic animals to mount the animals' heads above their fireplaces, wear their fur, or use their body parts as jewelry. In 2018, nearly 900 rhinos were poached for entertainment and social status. More than 1,000 elephants were killed for their ivory tusks between 2014 and 2017.

The conflict between those seeking to protect endangered

animals and others hoping to profit by poaching has also resulted in violence. Humans killed humans to kill animals; between 2009 and 2016, poachers murdered some 600 rangers protecting rhinos, elephants, and other wildlife in Africa. In the process, humans end up destroying animal habitats across the planet.

Tragically, we have also decimated fish populations and threatened island food supplies through overfishing. And we raise animals as if they are stalks of wheat, purely for consumption. Paradoxically, we treat domesticated animals like beloved family members.

Dire projections for the future of the planet suggest we must come to terms with this paradox. As a vegan of over a decade and a certified weight management specialist, with certificates in personal training and plant-based nutrition, I know humans can meet all their nutritional needs without consuming animal products. Why, then, do we do it?

FEAR

Another hard-wired instinct is the need for people to guard against imminent dangers. The perception of a life-threatening situation triggers a powerful flight-or-fight response in the brain. The amygdala, the part of the brain involved with emotions, sends distress signals to the hypothalamus, the brain's command center, which signals the heart to beat faster, muscles to tense, glands to produce sweat to cool the body, and breathing rates to increase in preparation to battle or flee. All of this happens in a split second.

Having a healthy appreciation for when to fight and when to run has kept our species alive. When combined with tribalism and violent tendencies, however, fear is weaponized, stifling human progress.

Millions of people are born into lives replete with fear in the forms of persistent traumatic stress, anticipatory stress, and vicarious traumatization. Unlike post-traumatic stress generally tied to an event or a defined time period, persistent traumatic stress is ongoing. For some people, poverty is a type of persistent traumatic stress. There are people who grew up poor and say they didn't realize they were poor as a kid. For me, poverty was a constant intrusion: I knew I was poor. And I hated it.

Anticipatory stress is an expectation that something bad will happen. Parents are often afraid, for example, to take their eyes off their kids in public, fearing harm may find them. Vicarious traumatization occurs when people identify with others' trauma, particularly a fellow tribe member. When former First Lady Michelle Obama disclosed feelings of depression after watching the video of George Floyd's killing and other Black victims, it resonated with other Black people who felt similar trauma.

Extreme fear causes false alarms; we see danger in places where there is none. Fear can cause us to withdraw and to relinquish hopes and dreams. Fear also can be used as a mechanism to manipulate others. Fear erects invisible but impenetrable barriers, making it difficult to form close relationships, particularly with individuals who have different beliefs, backgrounds, and experiences—other tribes.

To experience even one of these forms of stress is untenable. To experience all three is no way to live, especially not for the most advanced species on earth. It's the equivalent of a first responder living in a constant pandemic with no letup in sight.

WHERE DOES
THIS ALL LEAVE US?

The most fundamental challenge facing human beings in the twenty-first century is how to navigate a modern world with primitive and predatory instincts developed to survive life on the African savanna. Each of these instinctual traits—tribalism, a propensity for violence, and fear—is problematic. But it is their nexus that poses the greatest risk to the future of humanity.

The time has come for every person to pause and ask serious questions: Should the same weapons of mass destruction and drones used by military leaders also be in the hands of citizens? Why are we unable to make life-saving technologies and therapeutics available to people born into poverty? Who will benefit from such innovations as cloning to replace organs and advanced genetic manipulation to select the traits of unborn babies, and how will this be decided?

History doesn't leave a lot of room for optimism that humans will be responsible and compassionate enough to distribute these benefits equitably. Today, more than 7.8 billion people across the globe comprise a rich tapestry of colors, shapes, customs, traditions, and beliefs. Instead of celebrating these differences, tribalism is driving a wedge between them. Growing nationalism—perceiving the interests of one's own nation as separate from the interests of other nations or the common interests of all nations—is fomenting violent national and regional conflicts. Fear and intimidation have become preferred methods of "negotiation" across and within geographical boundaries.

We must redirect our tribal tendencies to embrace a broader, all-encompassing human tribe. We must understand that "us" and "them" are the same. We are all *Homo sapiens*. The more time we spend together and the more experiences we share across demographic lines, the more we can merge into the same global family.

Even though we are hard-wired from an evolutionary standpoint to do things that are neither in the interest of humanity nor the planet, fortunately, the brain is pliant. Evolution is constant and not fixed. People can adapt their thinking to stop perceiving visual differences as a default mechanism indicative of a threat when the situation is otherwise.

Moreover, unlike our early ancestors, each of us is a member today of many groups, from our friends and family members to work colleagues, schoolmates, teammates, political parties, and dozens of other "tribes." No "man" is an island.

If we are unable to figure out how to take care of each other and the planet, we all lose. Those big brains gifted to us by evolution will have failed to save us, and *Homo sapiens* will cede global dominance to some other species. Jellyfish are 550 million years old; they are certainly resilient. Maybe it is their time next.

Can we come together in a common goal of lasting equity and inclusion? Let's put it this way: we simply must. America today is an amalgamation of many "tribes" seeking common ground. Our shared history of racial turmoil—a history that continues to the present moment—positions us to see patterns that may otherwise be invisible. Understanding these patterns can guide us in transforming our differences into a cohesive force making *our* nation the singular entity it has long promised to be.

ENDNOTES

[1] Jonathan Aberman, "Are You Ever Curious? Here's Why," *The Washington Post*, July 17, 2017, https://www.washingtonpost.com/news/capital-business/wp/2017/07/17/are-you-ever-curious-heres-why/.

[2] Mark Muro, Robert Maxim, and Jacob Whiton, "Automation and Artificial Intelligence. How Machines are Affecting People and Places," Metropolitan Policy Program at Brookings, January, 2019, https://www.brookings.edu/wp-content/uploads/2019/01/2019.01_BrookingsMetro_Automation-AI_Report_Muro-Maxim-Whiton-FINAL-version.pdf.

[3] Oliver Cann, "Machines Will Do More Tasks Than Humans by 2025 but Robot Revolution Will Still Create 58 Million Net New Jobs in Next Five Years," World Economic Forum, September 17, 2018, https://www.weforum.org/press/2018/09/machines-will-do-more-tasks-than-humans-by-2025-but-robot-revolution-will-still-create-58-million-net-new-jobs-in-next-five-years.

[4] Justine Brown, et al., "Workforce of the Future: The Competing Forces Shaping 2030," PwC, May, 2018, https://www.pwc.com/gx/en/services/people-organisation/workforce-of-the-future/workforce-of-the-future-the-competing-forces-shaping-2030-pwc.pdf.

[5] Aberman, "Are You Ever Curious? Here's Why."

[6] Robert H. Frank and Philip J. Cook, *The Winner-Take-All Society: How More and More Americans Compete for Ever Fewer and Bigger Prizes, Encouraging Economic Waste, Income Inequality, and an Impoverished Cultural Life* (New York: Free Press, 1996).

[7] Peter Atwater, "The Gap Between the Haves and the Have-Nots Is Widening Sharply," *Financial Times*, June 10, 2020, https://www.ft.com/content/0ebfb7ca-a681-11ea-a27c-b8aa85e36b7e.

[8] David Berreby, personal interview, September, 2019.

[9] Ibid.

[10] "Lynching in America: Confronting the Legacy of Racial Terror," Equal Justice Initiative, 2017, https://lynchinginamerica.eji.org/report/.

[11] Kurt Terry, "Jesse Washington Lynching," Waco History, accessed January 25, 2022, https://wacohistory.org/items/show/55; Patricia Bernstein, "The Lynching of Jesse Washington," Lynching in Texas, accessed January 25, 2022, https://www.lynchingintexas.org/bernstein.

[12] José María Gómez, Miguel Verdú, Adela González-Megías, and Marcos Méndez, (2016) "The Phylogenetic Roots of Human Lethal Violence," *Nature*, *538*(7624), 233–237, https://doi.org/10.1038/nature19758.

[13] Melvin Konner, "A Bold New Theory Proposes that Humans Tamed Themselves," *The Atlantic*, March, 2019, https://www.theatlantic.com/magazine/archive/2019/03/how-humans-tamed-themselves/580447/.

[14] Erika Engelhaupt, "How Human Violence Stacks Up Against Other Killer Animals," *National Geographic*, September 28, 2016, https://www.nationalgeographic.com/science/article/human-violence-evolution-animals-nature-science.

[15] Konner, "A Bold New Theory Proposes that Humans Tamed Themselves."

[16] Ian Johnston, "Humans Evolved to Have an Instinct for Deadly Violence, Researchers Find," *The Independent*, September 28, 2016, https://www.independent.co.uk/news/science/human-evolution-violence-instinct-kill-murder-each-other-a7335491.html.

[17] Chris T. Darimont, Caroline H. Fox, Heather M. Bryan, and Thomas E. Reimchen, "The Unique Ecology of Human Predators," *Science*, 349(6250), 858–860, August 21, 2015, https://doi.org/10.1126/science.aac4249.

[18] Holly K. Ober, et al., (2011), "Identification of an Attractant for the Nine-Banded Armadillo, *Dasypus Novemcinctus*," Wildlife Society Bulletin, *35*(4), 425, https://doi.org/10.1002/wsb.79.

[19] "Poaching Statistics," Save the Rhino International, accessed January 25, 2022, https://www.savetherhino.org/rhino-info/poaching-stats/.

[20] Jani Hall, "Poaching Animals, Explained," *National Geographic*, February 12, 2019, https://www.nationalgeographic.com/animals/article/poaching-animals.

CHAPTER 2

AMERICAN EXCEPTIONALISM UNDER THE MICROSCOPE

Before Europeans settled in what was later named the United States of America, the pre-Clovis people had lived on the land for about 6,000 years. These non-Europeans crossed the Bering Straits connecting Siberia in Russia to present-day Alaska. Nearly 80 percent of Indigenous people today contain genetic traces of the original settlers, the real discoverers of America, making them truly Native Americans. Over time, they separated into as many as 160 different tribes, each with its own language, customs, and rich cultural traditions. Today, more than half of all US states are named after these tribes.

Like the European settlers who followed, Native Americans did what was needed to survive, leveraging human traits like curiosity and tribalism. Curiosity drove them to experiment with herbs as medicines and wild plants as foods. Tribalism enabled them to kill large mammals for nutrition, clothing, and shelter, and to keep families safe and preserve their culture. Violence was a part of life, resulting in sporadic conflicts with other tribes.

In popular entertainment forms like movies and television shows, Native Americans are often typecast as either savages or simple, peaceful people, grossly understating the complexity of their lives. Stereotypical images of Native Americans propounded these characterizations, evident most palpably in the logos of sports teams named for different tribes. These offensive impressions marginalized Native Americans as "lesser people," while rendering their true history and attainments invisible to the greater public. Fortunately, there has been a recent wave of name changes in sports, including the Washington football team, the Commanders, which used to be called a slur for Indigenous people.

Prior to the arrival of the first settlers, the land was theirs, but only in terms of its bounty, beauty, and spiritual sustenance. Little did they realize, until more Europeans arrived and established settlements and colonies along the Atlantic coast, that this land was a veritable gold mine, one the entire world would soon exploit.

Countries took turns searching for their pot of gold. Portuguese, Spanish, French, Dutch, and English explorers mounted expeditions to claim a share of the untold riches. Among them was the Italian seafarer Christopher Columbus, who sailed three ships to what he thought was the Indies, an old world, yet was credited with discovering a "New World." We now know that previous explorers like Leif Erikson had already "discovered" America, making Columbus not just a misguided explorer but a late one, as well. He died in 1506, still believing he had settled in Asia.

Columbus anchored first in the Bahamas, or Guanahani, as the native Taino people called the island. He described the Tainos in his journals as strong, kind, generous, and fine featured. Columbus subsequently sailed to what are today known as Cuba, the Dominican Republic, and Haiti, and continued to praise the kindness of the local inhabitants. "They brought us all they had in this world, knowing what I wanted, and they did it so generously and willingly that it was wonderful," he wrote.[21]

These depictions by Columbus were important in advertising throughout Europe the bountiful riches and subservient natives of the Americas, ultimately impelling a cavalcade of subsequent seafarers to conquer the Western Hemisphere, one tribe after another. Not just the weapons of battle killed off much of the Indigenous population; diseases like smallpox also wielded a sharp sword.

Columbus was anything but a kind benefactor, despite the comforting passages in his journal. After writing that there were few better people than the Tainos, he kidnapped ten of them to train as interpreters for the return trip to Spain. He subsequently sailed to the Bahamas with more ships and larger crews, with a singular purpose—subjugation. His men turned on the very people he called "wonderful," robbing, raping, murdering, and enslaving them. By 1510, nearly 90 percent of Tainos had died from disease and the physical toll of slavery, resulting in the demand for new sources of forced labor.[22] As the Tainos perished, the Atlantic slave trade from Africa emerged in 1518 to fill the yawning gap.

One hundred fifty years later, Columbus Day was designated an official federal holiday, during the height of the civil rights movement. Schoolchildren were taught about Columbus's heroic transatlantic explorations, but not his treatment of the Native people he had deemed kind and generous. After reexamining the historical record, several US states and cities no longer celebrate Columbus Day, preferring to honor the legacy of Indigenous people instead.

Many individuals were unhappy with the decision to redirect the observance toward Native people, suggesting it whitewashes history in the quest for political correctness. The truth is otherwise. To continue a wrongheaded tradition denigrates the people who settled here first. Did those countless lost lives not matter? Pause for a moment and imagine how insulting it is to ask Native Americans to celebrate the life of their enslaver, an inept navigator whose subsequent actions fomented the enslavement of African people.

Once Columbus opened the doors of the Americas to the world, explorers came from all over. For some, curiosity drove the voyage. For poor peasants struggling to survive in their home countries, emigration was a response to fear and desperation. Still others ventured west due to political oppression and/or religious persecution. What they all had in common was the search for a better life.

PROFIT RULES THE ROOST

Nevertheless, throughout this period of colonization, one thing motivated the governments, corporations, and religious institutions funding the expeditions—making a profit right from the start. In establishing the New World's first city, St. Augustine, Florida, in 1565, Spanish explorer Don Pedro Menendez de Aviles had visions of turning the region into a commercial empire.[23]

Pioneers like the Virginians in Jamestown in 1607 and the Puritans in Massachusetts Bay in 1630 brought with them the forerunners of modern-day capitalism, creating goods that were sold at competitive market prices, generating the capital needed to increase employment and pay taxes to government entities providing services like roads and schools, enhancing the quality of life.

Eager to profit from the untapped resources of the New World, capital flowed from European investors to early settlers hoping to carve out businesses and other commercial enterprises and provide a nice life for themselves and their families. In contrast to the overcrowded cities in Europe, the New World was sparsely populated and blessed with vast agricultural and mineral riches. The problem, from the settlers' perspective, was the Native people who inhabited this land.

To appease Native Americans, governments realized they needed to form alliances with Columbus's "Indians." Most were established by missionaries seeking to "convert" tribes to Christianity, another form of subjugation, albeit one vastly more humane than enslavement. But these alliances were outliers, and most tribes resisted pressures to convert to Christianity while others prepared for battle.

Since there weren't enough settlers to perform the grueling work of tending the land, another form of labor was needed. In 1619, English pirates hijacked a Portuguese slave ship bound for Mexico and captured approximately two dozen Africans to fill the void. The foundation for slavery in the American South was built on the backs of these people and countless others. From the standpoint of capitalism, free labor offered the extraordinary opportunity to widen business profit margins, making America's products less expensive to produce and sell in the global marketplace.

Spain initiated the practice of enslaving Africans, but other European nations soon joined the country in what would become the largest migration of people in history, albeit forced. Although Africans and Europeans had a long history of trading people and goods, the transatlantic slave trade reached new commercial heights—and inhuman lows. The irony of the American Revolution is that Americans fought for the ideals of freedom, independence, and their right to claim land, while simultaneously raiding Native lands and holding Africans as slaves.

Despite their harsh treatment by pioneers, both Africans and Native Americans fought in that war, in the hope that fighting would prove them worthy of personhood. Some Native American tribes fought on the American side, while others fought for the British, thinking it would halt territorial encroachment.[24] Africans, both free and enslaved, fought squarely on the American side. The first casualty of the war, another irony, was Crispus Attucks, whose parents were Black and Native American.[25]

Once America obtained its independence, these marginalized

groups were treated as lesser humans or less than human. As per the Three-Fifths Compromise, slave owners counted three out of five slaves for legislative representation and taxation purposes.

THE AMERICAN WAY

Like other specious individuals extolled in history books as great Americans, Daniel Boone's legacy is a mixed bag. Boone was hailed as a hero for ignoring British orders prior to the war and for carving a trail through Cumberland Gap to establish a permanent settlement in Kentucky.[26] Along the way, he and his minions stole huge tracts of land from Native Americans and Mexicans or entered into unscrupulous contracts achieving the same aims.

Hordes of people followed in Boone's footsteps and migrated westward. The idea that the "ends justified the means" became part of "The American Way"—the nationalist ethos that adheres to the principles of life, liberty, and the pursuit of happiness. The process of claiming occupied land was formalized during the period from 1812 to 1860, the "Age of Manifest Destiny," based on early pioneers' conviction they were destined by God to seize land to achieve the enlightened goals of democracy and capitalism.[27]

As time progressed, manifest destiny was redefined in terms of Whiteness. Poet Rudyard Kipling, who believed White people were at the top rung of the human hierarchy and had a natural responsibility to govern inferior people, captured this ideology in his poem, *White Man's Burden*.[28] Whiteness was a God-given gift, anthropologist

William V. Ripley[29] wrote in *The Races of Europe*, clearing up any confusion over who could and could not take advantage of this gift.

Andrew Jackson, America's seventh president, was a chief proponent of Manifest Destiny. In 1830, Jackson signed into law the Indian Removal Act, forcing Native Americans from their ancestral lands to federally designated Indian territory west of the Mississippi River. Predominantly White European immigrants were now free to settle 25 million acres, uninhibited by Native resistance.

In his annual address to Congress in 1833, Jackson denounced Native Americans as almost unhuman, stating, "They have neither the intelligence, the industry, the moral habits, nor the desire of improvement which are essential to any favorable change in their condition. Established in the midst of another and a superior race . . . they must necessarily yield to the force of circumstances and ere long disappear."[30]

Jackson's view differed from predecessors like George Washington, who believed Natives could be "civilized"—turned into decent White men if only they were introduced to Christianity, taught to read and write English, adopted a European lifestyle, and allowed to own property, including African slaves in some instances. By 1837, approximately 46,000 Native Americans from the southeastern states had been forced westward, culminating in over 4,000 deaths and mourned, to this day, as the "Trail of Tears."

By the end of the nineteenth century, the combination of European diseases and more than 1,500 US government–authorized attacks had resulted in the deaths of nearly 15 million Native Americans, the victims of wide-scale genocide.

I lived in Jacksonville, Florida, for seventeen years. An imposing statue of Andrew Jackson wearing a cape and sitting on a horse is on display at the end of Laura Street near Independent Drive. Jackson was a slave owner who also callously removed Native Americans from their tribal lands. Since the killing of George Floyd, the statue has been vandalized numerous times, yet it still stands in celebration of the man responsible for the Trail of Tears.

THE ORIGINAL SIN

Many scholars of slavery and economics believe America's dominant position on the world stage can be chalked up to slavery and the free labor it provided. Among them is Cornell University history professor, Edward Baptist, who argues in his 2014 book, *The Half Has Never Been Told: Slavery and the Making of American Capitalism*, that the forced migration of Africans to America and their subsequent subjugation were integral in establishing the US as a global economic power.

Until the abolishment of slavery in 1865, more than 12 million Africans had been kidnapped and shipped as slaves to North America, the Caribbean, and South America.[31] Southern plantation owners profited from the sale of sugar, cotton, rice, and tobacco that slaves planted and harvested. Financial institutions in the North provided the funding for the Southern plantations and turned a profit on their investments.

The global economy also prospered. Cotton picked by Black hands in the South was bought by textile makers throughout Europe to make and sell clothing across the world, stimulating European economies and sparking the Industrial Revolution. Merchants who provided goods and services to the wealthy classes benefiting from slavery across America and Europe similarly filled their pockets with these ill-gotten gains.

The key player in the global slave trade was the Royal African Company, a trading enterprise chartered in 1672 by England's royal Stuart family and London merchants. Its initial goal to colonize Africa was augmented to include the capture and sale of African people as slaves. The Royal African Company, which enjoyed a monopoly, shipped more African slaves to the Americas than any other entity, on the order of 5,000 slaves each year during the 1680s.[32] After it lost its monopoly in 1698, other companies entered the fray. Ultimately, some 450,000 Africans found their lives irrevocably altered, sold as slaves in North America.[33]

Although Congress outlawed the African slave trade in 1808, the domestic slave trade flourished, encompassing the descendants of the original slaves.[34] Many members, up until the 67th Congress in 1923, were sympathetic to slavery. In fact, according to the *Washington Post*, 1,715 former members of Congress owned slaves at some point in their lives.[35] The ability to continuously increase the slave population by "natural" reproduction ensured the free labor advantage would persist. I put quotes around the word "natural" because slave owners were permitted by states to systematically force enslaved individuals to reproduce, thereby filling the void created by the end of the transatlantic slave trade.[36] The plantation owners got what they wanted: exponential increases in slave numbers, despite the fact that half of the children died within their first year.

Slavery represents one of the clearest examples of the predatory instincts of human beings. Lynching, rape, violent beatings, and forced family separations were all aspects of life for Black people in the American South. The willingness to wreak violence and terror upon a group of people based entirely on their skin color demonstrates the enormous danger of tribalism and greed, if left unexamined and unconstrained. It should give us all pause that so many people across the globe could conspire to treat human beings like animals for nearly 200 years, until the Civil War ended this inhumane practice.

We continue to celebrate the wrong people as heroes today. Although tremendous pressure is being exerted, slave owners and people who fought in the Civil War to preserve slavery still have schools, streets, colleges, parks, cities, and government buildings named for them. Perhaps the most insulting aspect of these monuments is the fact they were largely erected between 1890 and 1950, as an ominous message to Black people fighting to achieve racial equality. The descendants of many of these memorialized individuals fight to preserve their honored place in history. Perhaps they were kind to their friends and family members, or donated money to noble causes. These acts of decency pale, however, when confronted with their malicious actions.

There has been much discourse around who should take their place in town squares. Who better to be heralded on pedestals across the entire United States than those who have spoken out against the evils of slavery and sought its eradication from 1830, the official date abolition began as a movement, onward?

EMANCIPATION AT LAST

Were it not for the growing abolition movement and its impact on the minds and hearts of people in the Northern states, the emancipation of Black slaves would have taken much longer. Between 1860 and 1861, eleven Southern states seceded over the issue of slavery, igniting the Civil War. Two years later, the Emancipation Proclamation freed individuals enslaved in the Confederate-held territory. The Civil War ended in 1865 with the ratification of the Thirteenth Amendment to the US Constitution, which outlawed slavery in the entire nation. But the systematic denigration of Black people persisted.

While Reconstruction (from 1865 to 1877) was a significant era in American history, its gains were hard-fought and fleeting, each triumph countered by a devastating setback. To the dismay of White Southerners, Black people experienced many significant social, political, and legal victories, opened businesses, held high-level elected positions, and began to acquire land.

Although the Fourteenth Amendment of the Constitution in 1868 granted citizenship to freedmen, Southern states could continue to deprive Black citizens of equal rights, as the amendment did not supersede federalism, or "states' rights."[37] To enforce this deprivation, in 1865, White veterans of the Civil War formed the Ku Klux Klan, a loosely affiliated White terrorist group whose sole aim was to maintain White supremacy in response to Black civil and political gains.[38]

The Fifteenth Amendment gave freedmen the conditional right

to vote in 1870. Five years later, the Civil Rights Act was passed, prohibiting racial discrimination in hotels and other public accommodations. To enforce both laws, the National Guard had to be deployed in the South. White southerners established Black Codes and vagrancy laws that made it possible for Black people to be arrested for being unemployed, in an era where many White people would not hire them. Black people could be jailed and forced into hard labor, another form of slavery.

In 1875, Congress overturned the Civil Rights Act. The same year, the immoral eugenics movement began, falsely identifying heredity as the cause of human behavioral and cultural differences. Two years later, the so-called Compromise of 1877 abruptly halted any and all progress Black people had made up until that time. Rutherford B. Hayes, who became president in a hotly disputed election, was forced to make the compromise, which entailed the removal of federal troops from the South, effectively ending Reconstruction and abandoning Black people to the political whims of the Southern states.[39]

One can only imagine what life, liberty, and the pursuit of happiness would be like for Black Americans today had Reconstruction continued. Instead, Black people confronted the systemic inequities and cruelties inflicted during the Jim Crow era that began in 1877. Legal segregation and acts of severe discrimination were perpetrated against Black people in education, housing, employment, public transportation, voting rights, and criminal justice—essentially every aspect of public and private life.

Not just federal and state governments are to blame for the unfair and inhuman conditions imposed on Black people. In *Plessy v. Ferguson* in 1896, the US Supreme Court declared segregation legal under the "separate but equal" formula, barring Black people from Southern public life and civil rights.[40]

Out of options and often in fear for their lives, Black people fled the South in growing numbers from 1916 to 1919. During the so-called "Great Migration," more than half a million Black southerners moved to northern cities in search of employment opportunities. Companies were eager to employ Black people at a fraction of the cost they paid White employees, effectively establishing a two-tiered wage system based entirely on skin color. Businesses chartered buses to recruit eager-to-work and cheaper-to-pay Black people, often to replace striking White workers. Predictably, the White workers took out their anger and frustration on struggling Black workers, who had no option other than to cross the picket lines.

These shrewd employment practices, coupled with the fact that Black people were starting to build middle-class lives for themselves, fomented anti-Black riots in northern cities, including my original hometown of East St. Louis, Illinois. Considered the worst case of labor conflict in the twentieth century, nearly two hundred Black people were killed during the 1917 riot and more than six thousand were left homeless.[41]

It was just one riot among many others. The summer and fall of 1919 saw at least twenty-five riots pitting angry White people against Black people in their segregated neighborhoods. The period became known as the "Red Summer" because of the volume of Black blood staining the streets.[42] Ironically, for all the pronouncements about patriotism declared by the rioters, the primary targets were

Black veterans trained to use firearms to fight for America during World War I, much like when vocal supporters of law enforcement attacked the police during the "insurrection" of 2021.

Successful Black communities were leveled by working-class White mobs during the decade that followed. The Roaring Twenties did not roar economically for Black people. A case in point is Tulsa, Oklahoma, where Black businesses and banks thrived. The city, one of the wealthiest Black communities in America, was known as "Black Wall Street." Based on a rumor about a Black man and a White woman, a White mob looted and burned thirty-five city blocks. Over 300 people died and another 800 were injured during the riot.[43] Following a false claim of a Black-committed crime in Rosewood, Florida, an event depicted in a 1997 movie by the same name, a White mob stormed the town and burned it to the ground. Although these Red Summer riots were started by White people, far more Black people were charged with an assortment of crimes. Equal protection under the law did not apply.

By 1930, two million Black people had migrated north.[44] This great migration had a tremendous impact on the demographic makeup of the country that can still be felt in today's largest cities. New York's Harlem, for example, evolved into a cultural Mecca. With Black backing, Franklin D. Roosevelt was reelected president in 1936. Black people switched from the Republican to the Democratic Party, becoming part of the New Deal Coalition.

But as the Great Depression settled over the land, the New Deal did little to improve the lives of Black people, relative to their White counterparts.[45] The 1935 Social Security Act, for instance, had a deleterious impact on non-White people, as it exempted agricultural workers and domestic servants from receiving old-age insurance. These individuals, by and large, were Black, Mexican, and Asian. The same year, Congress passed the Wagner Act guaranteeing workers' rights, but the law did not prohibit unions from racial discrimination, rendering such rights useless. Once again, tremendous optimism was replaced by immense despair.

AMERICA'S
MISSED OPPORTUNITY

A Second Reconstruction commenced at the end of World War II, when Black soldiers who fought valiantly in the war returned home and were promised federal financial aid through the G.I. Bill to help pay for college and graduate school, as well as low-cost mortgages and loans to start businesses, among other benefits. It was a hollow promise, however, as the bill was racially discriminatory. State and local Jim Crow laws and federal actions by departments overseeing housing and education ensured Black people did not receive commensurate benefits as White recipients. As historian Ira Katznelson at Columbia University described the G.I. Bill, it was "affirmative action" for White people.[46]

The G.I. Bill's array of federal government programs made available to veterans to subsidize affordable loans to buy homes and go to college were not doled out on an equal basis. For many White veterans, the postwar period was a threshold toward a better life for them and their families. White recipients were often the first in their families to go to college or own a home that became a major source of wealth in future years.

While Black people qualified for the programs in theory, in practice, they could not take advantage of them. The government introduced a national real estate appraisal system, later called "redlining," reinforcing and even enforcing the continuing development of "Whites only" suburbs, leaving Black people in inner cities. Despite the individual merit and work ethic of Black veterans, they were barred from buying homes in predominately White neighborhoods with higher real estate values.

Of the $120 billion in FHA mortgages backed by the federal government from 1934 to 1962, less than 2 percent went to people of color.[47] Not only did White veterans have the means to buy suburban homes, but their houses were used as collateral to fund the education of their children. This collateral has also been valuable in terms of transferring wealth. As much as 80 percent of an individual's lifetime wealth is accumulated through intergenerational transfers.[48]

Similar problems confronted Black veterans in education. In the postwar years, limited opportunities existed for Black people to attend predominately White colleges and universities. Consequently, many Black students enrolled in HBCUs—historically Black colleges and universities. Unfortunately, there was not enough supply of HBCUs to meet the demand among young Black students, putting thousands on wait lists.

Many White Americans deservedly identify the G.I. Bill as the instrument that forever changed the fate of their families. Yet many

White people are either unaware or dismissive of the restrictions that barred Black veterans from seizing the same opportunities. In some cases, the same people whose families benefitted from the G.I. Bill can be counted on to argue against government programs assisting disadvantaged people. The ironies multiply.

CONTINUATION OF
JIM CROW

Moving forward to 1948, the Democratic Party's nominating convention adopted a strong civil rights slate, resulting in Southern delegates walking out of the convention and forming the states' rights "Dixiecrat" party.[49] Worse was in store for Black people in the South. Life was not only difficult; it became increasingly dangerous.

Jim Crow laws and practices made life barely tolerable. "For Whites only" signs were affixed to restaurants, public restrooms, and even public drinking fountains. These malicious actions evoked many of the Founding Fathers' perceptions that Black people were inferior to White people. The miseries weren't confined to Southern states. Many factories in the North that had recruited Black workers relocated their facilities to the suburbs, where Black people were barred from owning homes and didn't have the financial means to commute great distances back and forth to work. Black people were caught up in a vicious cycle—forced into random periods of unemployment, Black people were denigrated by persistent stereotypes that condemned them as "lazy" and "lacking initiative."

Politicians took advantage of the ire of White people regarding the advancement of Black people in America. Political advisors like Lee Atwater, who architected what became known as the Southern Strategy, commented in a recorded interview in 1981, "You start out in 1954 by saying, 'N****, n****, n****.' By 1968 you can't say 'n*****'—that hurts you, backfires. So, you say stuff like, forced busing, states' rights, [cutting taxes] and you're getting so abstract. Now…all these things you're talking about are totally economic things and a byproduct of them is, Blacks get hurt worse than Whites."[50]

The Montgomery bus boycotts in 1955 and 1956 led to the passage of the Civil Rights Act in 1957, but conditions for Black people remained unacceptable. In the mid-1960s, a Third Reconstruction coalesced, but only after countless marches, sit-ins, boycotts, and bloodshed. The sheer audacity among Black people to expect equal rights and protections under the law resulted in jail, hospitalization, or even death. Congress passed yet another Civil Rights Act in 1964, prohibiting discrimination on the basis of race, color, religion, sex, or national origin. And still, the violence continued.

In March 1965, Dr. Martin Luther King Jr., future congressman John Lewis, and 600 other activists marched from Selma to Montgomery, Alabama, in protest of tactics preventing Black people from voting. As they crossed the Edmund Pettis Bridge, they were attacked by police officers in what would become known as Bloody Sunday. Public outcry over images of Lewis being senselessly beaten impelled President Lyndon Johnson to sign the Voting Rights Act of 1965. Black Americans finally seemed to have their own shot at the American Dream.

POST-CIVIL
RIGHTS MOVEMENTS

Legislators knew when they passed the Civil Rights Act of 1964 that it couldn't make up for past bias and discrimination that had robbed Black people of equal opportunity since 1619. The best-case scenario was that things wouldn't get worse. Then, affirmative action programs sprouted. In 1965, via Executive Order 11246, government agencies were required to address the discriminatory practices in their contracting, hiring, and college admissions. In subsequent years, companies were compelled to no longer discriminate against certain groups of people in their hiring, promotion, and termination decisions.

The mechanisms to enforce these laws were controversial then and remain so today, with critics labeling affirmative action as so-called reverse discrimination. Yet how can centuries of discrimination based on race be atoned for by using race as a factor to offer qualified people opportunities?

The results of affirmative action programs have been mixed for Black people overall but are more positive for women. These programs have helped 5 million minority members and 6 million White and minority women move up in the workforce.[51] Between 1974 and 1980, federal contractors added Black and female officials and managers at twice the rate of non-contractors as a result of affirmative action goals.[52]

For all the claims of reverse discrimination, a study by Wesleyan University suggests if every unemployed Black worker were to displace a White worker, less than 2 percent of White people would be affected—a marginal percentage at best. Furthermore, affirmative action pertains only to job-qualified applicants, not all applicants, "so the actual percentage of affected White people would be a fraction of 1 percent," the study states.[53]

Despite these eye-opening statistics, battles are being fought today over whether or not race can be used as a factor in offering admission to college. Without the programs, however, the enrollment of Black students in college would drop to below 2 percent, the same study states. The reasons are numerous and varied and have little to nothing to do with merit. For example, mediocre White students are given priority treatment by university admission processes that favor the children of wealthy alumni, whom they expect to return the favor in the form of donations, grants, and foundations. What about the golf, swimming, and crew scholarships that are sometimes doled out to country club White kids who could otherwise afford to pay tuition? The scholarships for these less popular sports are largely funded by the revenue raised from football and basketball, where many of the players are Black.

I often wonder why White people who sue universities that include race as a determining factor in admissions don't cite other White people whose family lineage and wealth, as opposed to student merit, are factored into their admission. In the workplace, why don't

White workers aim their anger at the mediocre White relatives of current employees who get hired over more qualified White applicants? The reason seems clear—racial prejudice.

If all discrimination ended today, its legacy has created gaps that will take great time and effort to close. When you give one group of people a 400-year head start or throw significant obstacles at another group of people over the same time period, the immediate attainment of parity is impossible. Few people—those who are exceptionally gifted or lucky, really—could make up ground lost over centuries in a single year, or several decades even. Most Black people won't have extraordinary intelligence, talent, or work ethic just as most White people won't have extraordinary intelligence, talent, or work ethic. Extraordinary means more than ordinary, more than average. Without some form of intentional intervention, average Black people have little more than a prayer of attaining extraordinary success in America.

WHO IS A
REAL AMERICAN?

Many people, White and Black, thought the historic election of Barack Obama in 2008 would become a turning point for race relations in America. To some degree, it was. Black children now knew it was possible to become anything they wanted to be, even if circumstances made it unlikely.

More than a decade later, Black people still suffer significant quality of life disparities when compared to White people. Black people earn less than their White counterparts at every level of education.[54] Black people continue to experience nearly double the unemployment rate of White people at every level of education. Redlining is no longer legal, but minority homebuyers still pay nearly half a billion dollars more in interest every year when compared to White borrowers with similar credit scores.[55] I might add that the best advice for Black people looking to get their homes appraised is for them to take down all the Black family photos in the home if they want to avoid being downgraded, based on the many stories cited in the news recently.

Tragically, due to the failed War on Drugs, nearly 80 percent of people incarcerated in federal prison and almost 60 percent of those in state prison for drug offenses are Black or Latinx, even though White people are more likely than Black people to use drugs and just as likely as Black people to sell drugs.

As bad as the story is for African Americans, the experience of Native Americans cannot be forgotten. Their population rates have diminished significantly after colonization, to under 7 million today. Economically, they endure the highest rate of poverty of any racial group in America.[56] While the American Dream has attracted people from all over the globe, it remains an unfair and often cruel place for the two groups that didn't come here of their own accord.

Every child has the right to dream their version of the American Dream and make it become real, irrespective of the color of their skin, where they were born, or how much money their parents have amassed. We all deserve a seat at the table, as Langston's Hughes classic poem, "I, Too," continues to urge.

I, too, sing America.

I am the darker brother.
They send me to eat in the kitchen
When company comes,
But I laugh,
And eat well,
And grow strong.

Tomorrow,
I'll be at the table
When company comes.
Nobody'll dare
Say to me,
"Eat in the kitchen,"
Then.

Besides,
They'll see how beautiful I am
And be ashamed—

I, too, am America.

Now I ask you, nearly a century after Hughes penned this powerful poem in 1926, are all who "sing America" treated and respected as actual Americans?

Not in the ideology of White supremacists, who are quick to point out that America was designed for White people. The awkward truth is they are correct. Few of the Founding Fathers, a group of predominantly wealthy, White plantation owners, intended America to be a haven for anyone other than White people.

While the Constitution was amended to provide legal privileges long denied to Black Americans, from an ideological standpoint, non-White Americans are still seen as "guests" to be tolerated. This notion is evident in today's immigration debates. Educated Europeans are the favored immigrants; Black and Brown people are to be barred.

When Black people seek to elucidate obvious inequities and injustices, they ironically become "un-American." Consider how many White people reacted when then-NFL quarterback Colin Kaepernick kneeled during the national anthem. They felt he disrespected "their" flag, but overlooked the fact that Black people have fought and died in every US war and helped build this country in successive generations. Kaepernick's ancestors earned that flag, but it belonged not to him.

Maybe a shift in thinking will follow a shift in language. We need new terminology to describe our status as full Americans. Putting the word "African" before "American" serves as an asterisk, relegating Black people to second-class citizenship. We don't call White people European American, nor should we call Black people African American.

I'd be ashamed to admit to Hughes that America has yet to equitably share the table. We still sing America even louder than before, shouting from the mountaintop, "We, too, are America." Our voices are hoarse but will not weaken. Until each of us listens to the plaintive cries and whispers of our fellow beings, America will remain a work in progress.

Despite incremental progress for Black people and other historically marginalized groups, issues of systemic racism, racial profiling, and police brutality fester in cities large and small. After the historic election of the nation's first Black president, Barack Obama, predictable backlash followed this remarkable achievement, repeating a familiar pattern. As of early 2022, the number of hate groups has since surged to over 838 according to the Southern Poverty Law Center, generating efforts to roll back equal protections under the law for Black Americans.[57]

Maybe change is upon us again. In 2020, vibrant protests erupted across cities and bold statements were issued from political and business leaders. And in 2021, the country's first woman Vice President, Kamala Harris, who happens to be both Black and Asian, took office. At the same time, there is a significant push to bury much of the history I have presented in this chapter. Fights are erupting all over the country at local school boards, with some White parents claiming that forcing their children to learn about the ugly aspects of American history would be damaging to them. We really owe it to our kids to educate them about this history, so they chart a path to a better future for all of us.

[21] Russell Freedman, "Coming to America: Who Was First?" NPR, October 8, 2007 https://www.npr.org/templates/story/story.php?storyId=15040888.

[22] "American Beginnings: 1492–1690, Enslaved Peoples," National Humanities Center, accessed January 25, 2022, https://nationalhumanitiescenter.org/pds/amerbegin/settlement/text6/text6read.htm.

[23] Matt Blitz, "The Oldest City in the United States," *Smithsonian Magazine*, September 3, 2015, https://www.smithsonianmag.com/travel/us-oldest-city-st-augustine-florida-180956434/#bfKQrzCq7hCWbiJp.99.

[24] Rebecca Beatrice Brooks, "Native Americans in the Revolutionary War," The History of Massachusetts Blog, November 15, 2018, https://historyofmassachusetts.org/native-americans-revolutionary-war/.

[25] "Crispus Attucks," Biography.Com, April 2, 2014, https://www.biography.com/military-figure/crispus-attucks.

[26] Robert F. Collins, *A History of the Daniel Boone National Forest, 1770–1970*, (California: University of California Libraries, 1975).

[27] Robert L. Beisner, *American Foreign Relations Since 1600: A Guide to the Literature* (Denver: ABC-CLIO, 2003).

[28] Paul Halsall, "Modern History Sourcebook: Rudyard Kipling, The White Man's Burden, 1899," Fordham University, January 26, 1996, https://sourcebooks.fordham.edu/mod/Kipling.asp.

[29] William Z. Ripley, (December 1, 1899). "The Races of Europe; A Sociological Study," *The American Historical Review*, 5(2), 325–329, https://doi.org/10.1086/ahr/5.2.325.

[30] Donald L. Fixico, "When Native Americans Were Slaughtered in the Name of 'Civilization,'" History, March 2, 2018, https://www.history.com/news/native-americans-genocide-united-states.

[31] Henry Louis Gates Jr., "How Many Slaves Landed in the US?" The Root, January 6, 2014, https://www.theroot.com/how-many-slaves-landed-in-the-us-1790873989.

[32] Thomas K. McCraw, "It Came in the First Ships: Capitalism in America," Harvard Business School: Working Knowledge, October 12, 1999, https://hbswk.hbs.edu/item/it-came-in-the-first-ships-capitalism-in-america.

[33] Gates Jr., "How Many Slaves Landed in the US?"

[34] Steven Mintz, "Historical Context: Facts about the Slave Trade and Slavery," Gilder Lehrman Institute of American History, accessed January 25, 2022, https://www.gilder lehrman.org/history-resources/teaching-resource/historical-context-facts-about-slave-trade-and-slavery.

[35] Julie Zauzmer Weil, Adrian Blanco, and Leo Dominguez, "More Than 1,700 Congressman Once Enslaved Black People. This Is Who They Were, and How They Shaped the Nation," *The Washington Post,* January 10, 2022, https://www.washington post.com/history/interactive/2022/congress-slaveowners-names-list/.

[36] Manning Marable, *How Capitalism Underdeveloped Black America: Problems in Race, Political Economy, and Society* (Boston: South End Press, 1999).

[37] Nell Irvin Painter, *Creating Black Americans: African-American History and Its Meanings, 1619 to the Present* (Oxford: Oxford University Press 2005).

[38] Jonathan M. Bryant, "Ku Klux Klan in the Reconstruction Era," *New Georgia Encyclopedia*, August 12, 2020, https://www.georgiaencyclopedia.org/articles/history-archaeology/ku-klux-klan-reconstruction-era.

[39] Painter, *Creating Black American.*

[40] Ibid.

[41] A. Moore, "8 Successful and Aspiring Black Communities Destroyed by White Neighbors," Atlanta Black Star, December 4, 2013, http://atlantaBlackstar.com/2013/12/04/8-successful-aspiring-Black-communities-destroyed-white-neighbors/4/.

[42] Richard Wormser, "The Rise and Fall of Jim Crow," Thirteen Media with Impact, accessed January 25, 2022, https://www.thirteen.org/wnet/jimcrow/stories_events_red.html.

[43] James S. Hirsch, *Riot and Remembrance: The Tulsa Race War and Its Legacy* (Boston: Houghton Mifflin Harcourt, 2002).

[44] Ronald Takaki, *A Different Mirror: A History of Multicultural America* (Boston: Back Bay Books, 1993).

[45] Painter, *Creating Black American.*

[46] Ira Katznelson, *When Affirmative Action Was White: An Untold History of Racial Inequality in Twentieth-Century America* (New York City: W. W. Norton & Company, 2006).

[47] "Uncle Sam Lends a Hand," PBS, 2003, https://www.pbs.org/race/000_About/002_06_a-godeeper.htm.

[48] "RACE—The Power of an Illusion," PBS, 2003, http://www.pbs.org/race/000_About/002_04-background-03-02.htm.

[49] Painter, *Creating Black American.*

[50] Gaius Publius, "Lee Atwater's Infamous "N*gger, N*gger" Interview," AMERICAblog Media, November 18, 2012, http://americablog.com/2012/11/audio-of-infamous-lee-atwater-interview-its-a-matter-of-how-abstract-you-handle-the-race-thing.html.

[51] Associated Press, "Reverse Discrimination Complaints Rare, Labor Study Reports," *The New York Times*, March 31, 1995, https://www.nytimes.com/1995/03/31/us/reverse-discrimination-complaints-rare-labor-study-reports.html.

[52] Ibid.

[53] Scott Plous, "Ten Myths About Affirmative Action," University of Illinois Springfield, September 10, 2014, https://www.uis.edu/aeo/wp-content/uploads/sites/10/2014/09/Ten-Myths-About-Affirmative-Action.pdf.

[54] "Median weekly earnings by educational attainment in 2014: The Economics Daily," US Bureau of Labor Statistics, January 23, 2015, https://www.bls.gov/opub/ted/2015/median-weekly-earnings-by-education-gender-race-and-ethnicity-in-2014.htm.

[55] Jessica Guerin, "Study: Minority Homebuyers Pay Higher Interest Rates," HousingWire, November 20, 2018, https://www.housingwire.com/articles/47456-study-minority-homebuyers-pay-higher-interest-rates/.

[56] "Native American Population 2021," World Population Review, 2021, https://worldpopulationreview.com/state-rankings/native-american-population.

[57] "Hate Map," Southern Poverty Law Center, accessed January 25, 2022, https://www.splcenter.org/hate-map.

CHAPTER 3

THE MODERN MYTH
OF MERITOCRACY

Since its inception, millions of people have immigrated to the United States to chase the American Dream, the ethos that equal opportunity is available to one and all to achieve their aspirations for a better life through work and determination. A survey by the Brookings Institution affirms that Americans are more optimistic than people in other nations, believing their effort, intelligence, and skill are the golden path to success and wealth.[58]

The American Dream is a noble ideal, but it certainly has not been equally attainable by different groups of people, evidenced by Black and Brown populations experiencing double the poverty rates of White people, as the table below from the US Census Bureau discloses.

Percentage in Poverty	
White	8.1%
Asian	10.1%
Hispanic	8.1%
White	17.6%
Black	20.8%
Men	10.6%
Women	12.9%
All	11.3%

Poverty rate by group.

What accounts for these differences in the attainment of success and wealth? The answer is complex, but two contributing factors are the fable of meritocracy and the reality of sheer chance.

Meritocracy is a social system in which a person's capabilities result in advancement, irrespective of wealth and family or social connections. Everyone likes a good Horatio Alger "rags-to-riches" tale of the individual who starts out life with nothing "but the clothes on his back," who defies odds and achieves extraordinary success through perseverance and tenacity. I refer to this concept as "organic" merit. Many books based on this narrative have become bestsellers, and Hollywood has made millions of dollars retelling the same plot again and again. While inspirational, novels and movies present an idealized version of reality. The truth is more nuanced.

Getting to the top in America is far from easy, unless you are born to it. The US ranks twenty-seventh among major economies in terms of social mobility (the movement up or down in financial circumstances related to the wealth of parents).[59] Only 4 percent of Americans raised in the bottom quintile of income distribution make it to the top quintile as adults.

A mere 8 percent of Americans reared in the top quintile of wealthy families fall to the bottom quintile as adults.[60] The question is this: did the 92 percent that remained in the top quintile work as hard as their forebears, or did they have the generational connections and money to sustain them whether they worked hard or not? I refer to this condition as "assumed merit" for two reasons. First, these individuals just take their role or assume their position in society. Second, others assume that rich people are smarter or more hard-working.

Conversely, when it comes to Black people who fail to rise above their basement income rankings, the reason typically given is their lack of initiative. I don't mean to dismiss the uplifting examples of people from humble beginnings who achieve renown and success. In such cases, many talented people were the beneficiaries of what I call "facilitated merit." Someone at some point in time recognized their talent or effort and gave them a boost that lifted their chances of future success. Others without this opportunity often remain stuck in an income class, regardless of personal initiative.

WORK HARDER THAN EVERYONE ELSE

I am not suggesting hard work doesn't matter. It is often a necessary but not sufficient attribute. Rather, effort and luck are a powerful elixir. As a Major League Baseball fan, my favorite players often were the athletes who succeeded despite their physical stature and gifts. For some reason, they had what it took to excel.

An example is Tommy Edman of the St. Louis Cardinals, my team. At five feet, nine inches tall and 180 pounds, Edman is not an imposing physical specimen. The average weight of a Major League Baseball (MLB) player is roughly 207 pounds, and the average height is about six feet, two inches.[61]

Edman played baseball at Stanford University. After his junior year, the Cardinals drafted him in the sixth round of the 2016 MLB draft. Fewer than 25 percent of players drafted in such a late round make it into the majors, starting and ending their careers in the minor league. Yet there was Edman in 2019, standing at the plate with the iconic Cardinal birds emblazoned on his bat. In true Tommy Edman fashion, once he had his opportunity with the team, he took advantage of it. He was the sparkplug that ignited the team through the playoffs, just a few games short of the World Series.

Few would argue Edman did not work hard or exhaust every ounce of power in his five-foot-nine frame. Yet it's doubtful sports fans would know his name today were it not for the influence of his father, a baseball enthusiast who played the game in college and later coached his son's high school baseball team. On the other hand, there are kids who grow up in families of coaches who don't excel at sports because they lack the work ethic for success even when the path is carved out for them.

Had Edman been unlucky enough to be born into a different family, his story might have turned out differently. Perhaps his work ethic would have led him to become successful at something else, but without his father's influence, would hard work alone have been sufficient for him to attain success in baseball? Consider the many hard-working Black kids who are unlucky enough to grow up in poverty without someone like Tommy Edman's father to guide and mentor them.

BE MORE TALENTED THAN EVERYONE ELSE

Tiger Woods has a complicated story, but I'll stick with the less controversial parts. It's not that Woods hasn't worked hard to become arguably the greatest golfer in history; his work ethic is well documented. However, few people would deny that his incredible talent was clearly evident as a child, well before he could spell the words "hard work." Tiger appeared on the Mike Douglas show hitting golf balls at age three and was featured in *Golf Digest* two years later.

Woods started winning tournaments as soon as he was eligible to compete. He won six Junior World Championships and three consecutive US Amateur titles, turned pro and became the fastest player in history to reach a ranking of number one on the PGA Tour. To date, he has amassed eighty-two tournament wins on the PGA Tour, tying him with the great Sam Snead. His win total surpasses the combined wins of the other top ten golfers on the PGA Tour today. Woods's fifteen victories in major tournaments trails only the legendary Jack Nicklaus, who has eighteen. Altogether, Tiger has an astounding seventeen Guinness World Records in golf, behind only Usain Bolt and Michael Phelps for the most of any athlete in a single sport.

There's no question Woods enjoys unparalleled talent and put strenuous effort into honing his craft, but what else might he have become were it not for his father Earl's golfing interest and enthusiasm? Like Tommy Edman's father, Earl Woods played a significant role in his son's success, introducing him to the sport at a very early age. He also served in the US Armed Forces, giving Tiger access to affordable golf facilities at military bases. In terms of Woods's professional golf career, he was extremely lucky to be Earl Woods's son.

Fate might have presented Tiger with a golf club through some other avenue, or he might have become a world class athlete at another sport, given his athleticism and work ethic. We can only speculate, but what we do know is that Earl Woods's passion for golf guided Tiger's early access to the sport that fueled his ultimate success.

What if Wolfgang Amadeus Mozart's father, a violinist, did not teach him basic notes on the harpsichord? What if Wayne Gretzky had not grown up in Canada, the birthplace of hockey? What if songwriter Lula Mae Hardaway, the mother of Stevie Wonder, hadn't helped him write his first compositions as a teenager? Good fortune is fortune, indeed. The most talented people in history were lucky enough to have a family or other connection that enabled them to exploit their talents.

BE MORE INTELLIGENT THAN
EVERYONE ELSE

Respected philanthropist Bill Gates achieved great wealth and influence as the co-founder and former CEO of Microsoft. At thirteen, Gates wrote his first software program. A few years later, he was a National Merit Scholar, scoring 1590 out of 1600 on the SAT. He subsequently attended Harvard University for two years, before dropping out to launch Microsoft, one of the world's most successful technology companies.

Gates was not just smart and ambitious; he, like Edman and Woods, was fortunate. As the son of a prominent lawyer and the grandson of a bank president, his family had the financial means to send him to the elite Lakeside Preparatory School outside Seattle. There, he was introduced to computers and software coding, at a time when most children his age had never even seen a computer, much less operated one.

Imagine if Gates had been born into a poor family living in public housing, with zero access to a computer, like so many Black kids in the US. His IQ might not have been enough to save him. Although studies suggest that 25 to 50 percent of people believe a person's IQ is a predictor of future income, they're wrong. According to Nobel Prize–winning economist James Heckman, less than 2 percent of a person's income is directly attributable to the individual's IQ.[62] Other factors—like being born into a family that can afford to send you to Lakeside Prep—are more indicative of future income.

I'm not suggesting that Gates, given his natural intelligence and tenacity, wouldn't have made an impact on the world had he not been born into privilege. That's impossible to know. Nor would I ever fault his parents for sending him to a great school that offered so many opportunities. Nevertheless, a line can be drawn from his parental lineage through everything else that followed in his life. He deserves full credit for the effort he put into his studies and his groundbreaking development of personal computers. But he was lucky to have been born in a family with wealth, influence, and connections to assure the best of all possible futures. As my former professor, Dr. Frank, argues in another of his books, *Success and Luck*, in competitive contexts, many have merit, but it is luck that separates the few who are wildly successful from the rest.[63]

THE BIRTH LOTTERY

Obviously, the notion of meritocracy is skewed, since success is heavily influenced by pre-existing factors beyond individual effort, talent, intelligence, and ambition. It is often facilitated. For those born at the bottom of the economic scale, there's a good chance of remaining poor.

Children born into lower-income families are significantly more likely to be low-income in adulthood than children born into higher-income families, according to a study by the Stanford Center on Poverty and Inequality.[64] The expected family income of children born to families in the ninetieth percentile of income is about three times that of children born to families at the tenth percentile of income.[65] Yet their lack of success is often attributed to a perceived lack of effort, talent, or intelligence. Just as the wealthy enjoy assumed merit, the poor experience assumed unworthiness.

As Heckman described it, "the accident of birth is the greatest source of inequality in America today. Children born into disadvantage are, by the time they start kindergarten, already at risk of dropping out of school, teen pregnancy, crime, and a lifetime of low-wage work."[66]

Wealth breeds wealth; poverty breeds poverty. Wealthy people buy homes that appreciate. They invest their money and watch it grow. They have access to quality healthcare and can afford medical bills. They send their kids to private schools and pay for tutoring, music lessons, and test prep courses. Their children go to the best colleges, often on a "legacy" admissions basis, and are given the financial support for room, board, and social activities. Wealth and connections are invaluable, made palpably clear by the widespread revelations in 2020 of six-figure bribes paid by unscrupulous, wealthy, and celebrity parents to elite universities to admit their undeserving children, at a lifelong cost to the students who merited admission.

The cycle continues to spin in their favor. Once children of wealthy families graduate, they have little or no debt. Thanks to family connections and the magnetism of a diploma from an elite university, they're offered plum jobs and high salaries and benefits, augmenting their wealth. In turn, this makes it easier to put a down payment on a nice house in a "good" neighborhood. Even if they later make a dumb decision and break the law, they can afford a high-priced attorney to keep them out of jail. Bizarrely, in the high-profile criminal case against Ethan Couch, a wealthy teen who killed four people while driving intoxicated, the defense successfully offered "affluenza" as a justification for Couch to avoid jail time.[67]

THE LOSERS OF THE BIRTH LOTTERY

Poor people's problems begin in the womb. Poor people must live in government-subsidized substandard housing. They have no money to invest. Often, they take risks to "earn" their reward, spending what little they have at casinos or playing the lottery. They can't afford a catastrophic medical event or expensive life-saving medications.

If they have children, they must decide to either continue working or receive welfare, given the cost of child care. Living in struggling neighborhoods, they send the kids to failing neighborhood schools, where teachers are overwhelmed and supplies are wanting. They can't afford extracurricular activities, assuming these opportunities even exist. If they send their children to college, they or their kids must assume substantial debt obligations. Upon graduation, their children must fend for themselves to find affordable housing, with few options other than to stay where they currently reside. That's the cycle for them, spinning in another direction.

While it is terrible to be born poor in America, it is even worse to be born poor *and* Black in America. Black babies have significantly worse life outcomes than White babies do, if they survive birth at all. The infant mortality rate for non-Hispanic Black people is more than double (11.4 deaths per 1,000 live births) that of non-Hispanic White people (4.9 deaths per 1,000 live births).[68]

The common assumption is that this difference is a result of risky maternal behaviors. The issue is far more complex. Black women are less likely to smoke during pregnancy, for instance, but those Black women who did not smoke during pregnancy still had higher infant mortality than White women who smoked.[69] There is no evidence of greater alcohol or drug use among pregnant Black women than among pregnant White women, but that doesn't seem to matter either.[70] Moreover, Black women who initiated prenatal care in the first trimester still had higher rates of infant mortality than did White women, who had late or no prenatal care at all.[71] In fact, across forty-six different risk factors, there is only a 10 percent variance in birth weight in babies born to White and Black women.[72]

What accounts for the other 90 percent? Scientific research strongly suggests a baby's experiences in the womb can lead to negative health consequences later in life.[73] The fetus responds to stimuli in the womb, such as the mother's stress hormones triggered by racism, poverty, and fear. The fetus adapts physiologically to the hormones, putting it at risk of stress-related pathologies causing postnatal chronic health issues.[74]

We continue to learn more about the impact of stress over a lifetime. Previous research on infant mortality assumed that life-long chemical and psychological stressors could be erased during the nine months of pregnancy. They're not. This helps explain why infant mortality rates are still higher for Black women who eat a well-balanced diet, regularly exercise, and manage their stress during pregnancy. As Black children grow up, the ZIP codes where they live play a role in their lives. The ZIP codes comprising the most racially and ethnically segregated cities in America have the lowest rates of life expectancy.[75]

While the children of all poor families must contend with air pollution and other environmental toxins, a lack of access to healthy food and quality medical care, and subpar educational opportunities, Black children still have it worse. In 99 percent of neighborhoods in which Black boys and White boys grow up with comparable levels of family income and attend the same neighborhood K–12 schools, Black boys will earn less in adulthood than their White counterparts.

While income gaps between White and both Latinx and Asian American people are shrinking, this is not the case for Black people.[76] The gulf between the incomes of the median White family and the median Black family is immense—nearly ten to one.[77]

The cycle spins on and on—one way for White families and the other way for Black families.

- Children born to White parents with a college degree earn nearly three times the median income of children of non-White parents with a college degree and enjoy a net worth fourteen times greater than the children born to non-White parents without a college degree.
- White children with no college degrees born to parents with no college degrees have a net worth five times that of non-White children with no college degree born to parents with no college degree.

- White children who don't have a college degree born to parents that have college degrees have a net worth more than four times that of non-White children without a college degree born to parents with them.[78]

DOMINATE
EVERYONE ELSE

There is one other way some White people have achieved success—through sheer and often brutal force. Unfortunately, the idyllic view of the American Dream downplays or disregards the fact that success can be attained through savage violence and unsurpassable power.

Wealthy and powerful people have consistently demonstrated the capacity for rapacity through historic actions, like eminent domain, where financial success is attained through unscrupulous tactics at the expense of vulnerable populations. Yet these predatory instincts have not disappeared.

Evidence of brute power was on display leading to the 1998 Master Settlement Agreement signed by the nation's largest tobacco corporations with the attorneys general of forty-six states, requiring the companies to pay a minimum of $206 billion to defray the costs of wide-ranging health issues caused by cigarette smoking. The companies buried the harms of nicotine from the public for decades and directly marketed and advertised their products to young people as a necessary component of the "good life."

These tactics hit already vulnerable populations hardest.

- The types of cigarettes that are hardest to quit, menthols, are preferred by three times more Black people (77.4 percent) than White people (23.0 percent).[79]
- Lower income cigarette smokers suffer more from diseases caused by smoking than do smokers with higher incomes.[80]
- Secondhand smoke exposure is higher among poor people and those with less education.[81]
- Tobacco companies often target their advertising campaigns toward low-income neighborhoods and communities.[82]

Once again, irony abounds. Manufacturers of vapes, a product promoted as a way to wean smokers off cigarettes, studied and copied the tobacco industry's advertising tactics, resulting in 2,400 lung injuries and fifty-two deaths in 2019.[83] Vape manufacturers were criticized for using enticing flavors to lure young people into a nicotine addiction. At the time, more than 40 million people were active users of the nicotine-based products, including one in five high school students.[84] The good news is that vaping among US youths fell in 2020 for the first time in three years.[85]

Far more devastating is the role that Purdue Pharma and the family that controls the company, the Sacklers, had in creating and cultivating the nation's opioid crisis. Consistent with other studies regarding poverty and opioid overdose mortality, compared to people from the most affluent households, those living under the poverty line had higher risk of fatal opioid overdose.[86] Thousands of cities, towns, Native American tribes, state attorneys general, and other plaintiffs have filed civil cases against Purdue Pharma and other opioid manufacturers, distributors, and pharmacies. Due to the COVID-19 pandemic, these cases, considered the most complex litigation in American history, have been delayed. Settlement figures floated in the media exceed $25 billion, a mere pittance of the more than $630 billion the crisis has cost the US economy.[87] Meanwhile, in 2020, a federal judge approved a landmark $8.3 billion to settle its criminal and civil investigations with the company and civil settlement with the Sackler family.[88] In late 2021, the settlement was overturned, giving victims the right to sue the family directly.[89]

As of this writing, Facebook is dealing with its own crisis. A whistleblower has accused the social media giant of hiding internal research that outlined its harms to young people, as well as its role in fomenting hate and conspiracy theories.

Not just Corporate America is guilty of generating riches at the expense of vulnerable Americans. They're joined by white-collar criminals, human traffickers, slum lords, and street drug dealers, all believing the ends justify the means in the American Way. Nothing will change until we come to terms with the fact that hard work, talent, and intellect are not the primary keys to success—certainly not for everyone.

The collective belief in meritocracy is not only misleading but also marginalizes the well-being of vulnerable people by making them believe in a bogus principle—the idea that everyone has an equal shot of achieving the same high-quality existence. If they fail in this attainment, they rationalize it's their own fault; they just didn't stack up.[90] In turn, this often causes feelings of low self-esteem, anxiety, and depression.[91]

Paradoxically, a belief in meritocracy has the opposite effect for many wealthy individuals, resulting in higher self-esteem and an unwillingness to accept their success was driven by factors beyond their own control. Regrettably, such people are less likely to advocate for legislative policies that level the playing field. In fact, meritocracy makes people more selfish and less self-critical, as well as more apt to demonstrate discriminatory behavior.[92]

To illustrate how positive conditions create and reinforce positive outcomes for wealthy White people while negative conditions create and reinforce negative outcomes for poor Black people, I have created a model of self-sustaining outcomes.

Wealthy Whites	The System is Designed to Benefit You	Generous
Middle-Class and Poor Whites	The System is Neutral Towards You	Ambivalent
Wealthy and Middle-Class Blacks	The System is Designed to Disadvantage You	Wary
Poor Blacks	You are Blamed for the the Broken System	Hostile

Wealthy White People represent a small but incredibly influential group. The current system—tax loopholes, investment opportunities, valuable connections, access to top-notch education, etc.—is designed to benefit them. Put simply, the systems, structures, and institutions that shape their lives are Generous. These are the winners of the birth lottery. These individuals are admired and get the benefit of assumed merit.

Middle-Class and Poor White People is the cohort where

most White people find themselves. This is the group that generally balks at the notion of white privilege. That's understandable; the system doesn't give them anything. They lack the financial means of the wealthy White cohort, but they nonetheless have what I call the "Luxury of Independence," as they escape the predetermined future of other groups. They must compete. They can work hard or use their talent or intelligence to accumulate capital, separating themselves from their peers. While the system doesn't advantage them, it also doesn't disadvantage them. Wealthy White people are ambivalent to people in this cohort achieving high levels of success. If someone in this group makes it, that's great; if they don't make it, that's okay. They are not going to reduce the country club membership fee for someone just because they are a hard worker.

Wealthy and Middle-Class Black People are in a precarious situation. Even though they have "made it," they are constantly reminded that the system isn't designed for them. Former President Trump, for instance, famously (and erroneously) said that a well-educated Black person has more advantage than a well-educated White person. It is common for White people to lament the opportunities lost to them because of affirmative action or diversity programs compelling employers to hire Black people. This is bunk for an obvious reason: if Black people took jobs away from more qualified White people at a significant level, why do Black people remain dramatically underrepresented in the workforce and especially in management levels?

Not only does the system give Black people in this cohort no advantages, it disadvantages them compared to their White counterparts. Regardless of their background, experience, talent level, test scores, etc., Black people are penalized in the hiring process, as studies routinely demonstrate. How many of these studies proving present-day racial discrimination in hiring do we need to see before we acknowledge that such discrimination is still occurring?

If the system has been shaped by racial bias against Black people, then anyone who is Black is subject to those biases. A wealthy, educated Black man walking down the street will be subject to the same biases to which any other Black person would be subject. Racist people don't take the time to interview Black people to determine their education, income, or work ethic before they decide to discriminate against them. Even in situations where there is an evaluation, the bias often still remains. For instance, as mentioned earlier in this chapter, successful Black people are often saddled with higher interest rates than White people with the same credit scores. Banks are wary of Black people's perceived abilities to make good on their debt obligations.

Poor Black People are the real losers of the birth lottery. Not only does the system disadvantage them, but they are blamed for society's problems. Some middle-class and poor White people contend that poor Black people drain government resources. They feel their taxes would be lower and they would have more employment opportunities were it not for "lazy Black people" and the entitlements they receive. This stigmatized cohort includes the mythical "welfare queen" and individuals engaged in so-called Black-on-Black crime. Black people in other cohorts often try to distance themselves from this group and contend they lack the values necessary for success.

Having grown up in this cohort, I have some personal experience with what it feels like to be a target of such hostility. I was just a kid, but I could read about and hear the criticisms expressed about people in my situation. Much of it could not have been further from the truth. For example, most Black people are not in jail and most people in jail are not Black. Most Black murder victims are killed by Black people, but most White murder victims are killed by White people. Yet who ever complains about "White-on-White" crime? Moreover, most Black people are not poor and most poor people are not Black.

Given our relatively low numbers in the population, Black people are not draining the system. As for the people who play out some of the stereotypes, given everything we know about human psychology, we should not be surprised when Black people demonstrate self-destructive behaviors. Treat people like animals for so long, and they start to believe it. Think hard about someone willing to pull out a gun and shoot someone in the streets. They know they'll likely be shot or thrown in jail for a very long time. Not only do they lack empathy for the lives of their victims, but they care little about their own lives. Society must reach out to help young people in these situations before they commit violent crimes, and not threaten or belittle them. They have little hope to progress in a system that wasn't designed for them to achieve any real level of success. I'd love to see a White police chief get on television and tell the young, struggling Black people in their communities that they love them and don't want them to throw away their future. What impact could they make by acknowledging how hard life is for them and offering ways the police can help on the front end before kids end up in situations where they feel compelled to commit crimes?

The good news is, our current moment of reckoning has ignited a greater will for change. That change must begin with us setting aside old notions of success and how it must be achieved. We must focus on what is probable instead of idealizing what is possible. We must use our collective energies to shift the probabilities in favor of equal opportunity for everyone, rather than conditions at birth predicting life outcomes. In order for hard work, talent, and intelligence to matter, the game can't be rigged from the start.

[58] Julia B. Isaacs, "International Comparisons of Economic Mobility," The Brookings Institution, July 2016, https://www.brookings.edu/wp-content/uploads/2016/07/02_economic_mobility_sawhill_ch3.pdf.

[59] "Global Social Mobility Index 2020: Why Economies Benefit from Fixing Inequality," World Economic Forum, January 19, 2020, https://www.weforum.org/reports/global-social-mobility-index-2020-why-economies-benefit-from-fixing-inequality.

[60] "Pursuing the American Dream: Economic Mobility Across Generations," The Pew Charitable Trusts, July, 2012, https://www.pewtrusts.org/~/media/legacy/uploadedfiles/pcs_assets/2012/PursuingAmericanDreampdf.pdf.

[61] "Baseball Players All Shapes and Sizes," We Are Fanatics, September 10, 2018, http://wearefanatics.com/baseball-players-shapes-sizes/.

[62] Faye Flam, "Personality Has Greater Impact on Success than IQ, New Research Suggests," The Independent, August 7, 2017, https://www.independent.co.uk/news/science/personality-iq-success-wealth-factors-determining-prospects-intelligence-careers-james-heckman-national-academy-sciences-a7880376.html.

[63] Robert H. Frank, Success and Luck: Good Fortune and the Myth of Meritocracy (Princeton: Princeton University Press, 2016).

[64] Clifton B. Parker, "A High-Stakes Birth Lottery in the US, Stanford Researchers Say," Stanford University, July 24, 2015, https://news.stanford.edu/2015/07/24/economic-mobility-study-072415/.

[65] Pablo A. Mitnik and David B. Grusky, "Economic Mobility in the United States," The Pew Charitable Trusts and the Russell Sage Foundation, July, 2015, https://www.pewtrusts.org/~/media/assets/2015/07/fsm-irs-report_artfinal.pdf.

[66] John Komlos, "In America, Inequality Begins in the Womb," PBS NewsHour, May 20, 2015, https://www.pbs.org/newshour/economy/making-sense/america-inequality-begins-womb.

[67] Jessica Luther, "Affluenza: the Latest Excuse for the Wealthy to Do Whatever They Want," The Guardian, December 15, 2013, https://www.theguardian.com/commentisfree/2013/dec/15/affluenza-texas-dui-ethan-couch.

[68] "Infant Mortality," Centers for Disease Control and Prevention, accessed September 10, 2020, https://www.cdc.gov/reproductivehealth/maternalinfanthealth/infantmortality.htm.

[69] T. J. Mathews, Marian F. MacDorman, and Fay Menacher, (January 30, 2002,) "Infant Mortality Statistics from the 1999 Period Linked Birth/Infant Death Data Set," National Vital Statistics Reports, 50(4):1–28, https://pubmed.ncbi.nlm.nih.gov/11837053/.

[70] Gopal K. Singh and Stella M. Yu, (1995), "Infant Mortality in the United States: Trends, Differentials and Projections, 1950 through 2010," *American Journal of Public Health*, 85, 957–964.

[71] Mathews, "Infant Mortality Statistics."

[72] Robert L. Goldenberg, et al., (1996), "Medical, Psychosocial, and Behavioral Risk Factors Do Not Explain the Increased Risk for Low Birth Weight Among Black Women," *American Journal of Obstetrics and Gynecology, 175*(5), 1317–1324. https://doi.org/10.1016/s0002-9378(96)70048-0.

[73] Michael C. Lu and Neal Halfon, (2003), "Racial and Ethnic Disparities in Birth Outcomes: a Life-Course Perspective," *Maternal and Child Health Journal, 7*(1), 13–30, https://doi.org/10.1023/a:1022537516969.

[74] "Fetus to Mom: You're Stressing Me Out!" WebMD, accessed January 25, 2022, https://www.webmd.com/baby/features/fetal-stress.

[75] Jamie Ducharme and Elijah Wolfson, "Your ZIP Code Might Determine How Long You Live—and the Difference Could Be Decades," *Time*, June 17, 2019, https://time.com/5608268/zip-code-health/.

[76] "Racial Disparities in Income Mobility Persist, Especially for Men," Opportunity Insights, accessed January 25, 2022, https://opportunityinsights.org/race/.

[77] Lydia DePillis, "America's Wealth Gap is Bigger than Ever," CNNMoney, November 3, 2017, https://money.cnn.com/2017/11/03/news/economy/wealth-gap-america/index.html?iid=EL.

[78] Lydia DePillis, "The Financial Impact of Winning (and Losing) the Birth Lottery," CNNMoney, March 6, 2018, https://money.cnn.com/2018/03/06/news/economy/wealth-gap-birth-lottery/index.html.

[79] "Tobacco Use in Racial and Ethnic Populations," American Lung Association, October 14, 2020, https://www.lung.org/quit-smoking/smoking-facts/impact-of-tobacco-use/tobacco-use-racial-and-ethnic.

[80] "Tobacco and Socioecenomic Status," Campaign for Tobacco-Free Kids, November 3, 2021, https://www.tobaccofreekids.org/assets/factsheets/0260.pdf.

[81] "Vital Signs: Disparities in Nonsmokers' Exposure to Secondhand Smoke—United States, 1999–2012," Centers for Disease Control and Prevention, February 6, 2015, https://www.cdc.gov/mmwr/preview/mmwrhtml/mm6404a7.htm.

[82] "The Health Consequences of Smoking—50 Years of Progress: A Report of the Surgeon General," Centers for Disease Control and Prevention, 2014, https://pubmed.ncbi.nlm.nih.gov/24455788/.

[83] Jasmine Aguilera, Jamie Ducharme, and Elijah Wolfson, "Vaping-Related Illnesses and Death Toll Continue to Rise, But the Outbreak May Be Nearing an End," *Time*, January 9, 2020, https://time.com/5692387/vaping-related-death-toll/.

[84] Stephen Dubner, "The Truth About the Vaping Crisis (Ep. 398)," *Freakonomics*, November 20, 2019, https://freakonomics.com/podcast/vaping-nicotine/.

[85] William Wan, "Vaping Among Teens Falls for the First Time in Three Years," *The Washington Post*, September 9, 2020, https://www.washingtonpost.com/health/2020/09/09/teen-vaping-rates-fall/.

[86] Sameer Imatiaz, Charlotte Probst, and Jürgen Rehm, "Substance Use and Population Life Expectancy in the USA: Interactions with Health Inequalities and Implications for Policy," Drug and Alcohol Review, April, 2018, https://pubmed.ncbi.nlm.nih.gov/29737615/.

[87] Meryl Kornfield, "Coronavirus Pandemic Delays Opioid Court Trials," *The Washington Post*, December 26, 2020, https://www.washingtonpost.com/health/2020/12/26/coronavirus-opioid-trials/.

[88] Brian Mann, "Federal Judge Approves Landmark $8.3 Billion Purdue Pharma Opioid Settlement," *NPR*, November 17, 2020, https://choice.npr.org/index.html?origin=https://www.npr.org/2020/11/17/936022386/federal-judge-approves-landmark-8-3-billion-purdue-pharma-opioid-settlement.

[89] Brendan Pierson, Mike Spector, and Maria Chutchian, "US Judge Tosses $4.5 Billion Deal Shielding Sackers from Opioid Lawsuits," *Reuters*, December 17, 2021, https://www.reuters.com/business/judge-tosses-deal-shielding-purdues-sackler-family-opioid-claims-2021-12-17/.

[90] Erin B. Godfrey, Carlos E. Santos, and Esther Burson, "For Better or Worse? System-Justifying Beliefs in Sixth-Grade Predict Trajectories of Self-Esteem and Behavior Across Early Adolescence," Society for Research in Child Development, June 19, 2017, https://srcd.onlinelibrary.wiley.com/doi/full/10.1111/cdev.12854.

[91] Melinda D. Anderson, "Why the Myth of Meritocracy Hurts Kids of Color," *The Atlantic*, July 27, 2017, https://www.theatlantic.com/education/archive/2017/07/internalizing-the-myth-of-meritocracy/535035/.

[92] Clifton Mark, "A Belief in Meritocracy is Not Only False: It's Bad for You," Princeton University Press, June 22, 2020, https://press.princeton.edu/ideas/a-belief-in-meritocracy-is-not-only-false-its-bad-for-you.

PART 2

DIVERSITY, EQUITY, INCLUSION, AND BELONGING

CHAPTER 4

FROM *HOMO SAPIENS* TO *MISERATOR HOMINIBUS*

From an evolutionary standpoint, human beings have evolved to commingle technical brilliance with an enduring predatory instinct. Due to the continuing rapacity of some powerful and wealthy individuals and the socioeconomic and planetary harms left in their wake, correcting this concurrence is imperative. Evolution is slow and will not save us. We must proactively shape our collective destiny now.

This ethical and moral future can only be seized with a genuine love for all of humanity. Empathy must be at the core of a new society. We must evolve from "wise men," *Homo sapiens*, to "compassionate people," *Miserator hominibus.* Our institutions must be reimagined and reengineered to ensure every person is treated with respect and care. Each life must be valued equally. A Black child born into poverty in East St. Louis must have the same value as a White child born into wealth in Bel Air.

Children do not choose their parents, their sex assigned at birth, their skin color, their economic class, or their religion. Yet these conditions indelibly mark their fate. The timing is critical, as the gap between the "haves" and "have nots" widens, especially in the United States. The country, arguably the leader of the free world, is nonetheless home to the largest income gap among the Group of Seven (G7) countries.

Since 1980, the income of the top 10 percent of earners in the US has increased 39 percent. In 2020, these individuals earned more than 12.6 times the income of the remaining 90 percent of the population.[93] According to the Federal Reserve of St. Louis, the top 1 percent of income earners now holds 30.5 percent of the nation's wealth, up from 28.6 percent in 2010. The bottom 50 percent of income earners holds 1.9 percent of the nation's total wealth, up from 0.5 percent in 2010.[94]

Even during crisis times, the rich continue to get richer. During the Great Recession following the financial crisis of 2008, the net worth of the top 20 percent of income earners in the US actually rose, while all others endured some measure of economic duress. During COVID-19, many companies have reported record profits, and the wealth gap has increased between billionaires and everyone else.[95]

COVID-19 also illuminated the political divide in ways no other crisis has across American history. Many on the extreme right blasted the need to wear masks or vaccine mandates as an affront to their Constitutionally guaranteed rights to freedom. Threats of violence and actual acts of violence were perpetrated against members of school boards, flight attendants, and Asian Americans, blamed for a virus that originated in China.

We cannot meet the enormous challenges of the present with the basic instincts and default wiring of 200,000 years ago. We must move from a system that marginalizes vulnerable populations to one that protects them. Here's a look at the shift we need to make in society.

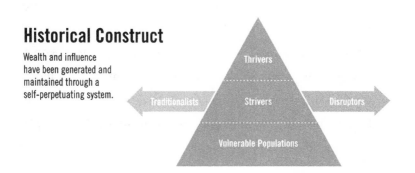

Historical Construct

Wealth and influence have been generated and maintained through a self-perpetuating system.

Thrivers

Traditionalists · Strivers · Disruptors

Vulnerable Populations

Future Construct

Society progresses through an interdependent system where everyone has value and contributes at various levels throughout their lives.

Again, a small percentage of individuals are experiencing extraordinary success while the middle class is feverously battling it out to keep from falling into the bottom rungs of society where people are struggling with issues like homelessness and hunger. To move society forward, the hierarchy in which a handful of Thrivers can easily grab the brass ring must give way to one in which all people have an equal shot to live life to its fullest.

VULNERABLE HUMANS

Children, the elderly, people with mental and physical illnesses or challenges, and those born into poverty must be treated with respect and recognized for their humanity. Not only are these individuals often overlooked, but they are frequently victims of abuse at the hands of the very people who are supposed to take care of them. Part of the problem is the pay structure of the jobs that provide services for them. Some people are drawn to these positions out of compassion, but it is difficult to get talented, dedicated people to do these jobs because the salaries are so low. In many states, public school teachers are paid an abysmal $40,000 per year, although a living wage in the US for a family of four is more than $68,000.[96] Daycare workers have it worse, earning an average of $22,038 per year.[97]

As a society, we must rally around our vulnerable citizens, especially the nation's children who didn't choose their parents or birth circumstances. And we must be mindful not to blame the parents too harshly because, in many cases, the parents grew up in the same situations and never got the experiences they needed to provide better opportunities for their kids.

From a workplace standpoint, we need to think of the working poor as vulnerable. To provide some security for them requires a living wage—something not in reach of the working poor. Approximately 38 million people in the US, nearly 12 percent of the population, lived below the official poverty level in 2018. Roughly 7 million of them are characterized as the "working poor" by the US Bureau of Labor Statistics.[98]

Disruptors

As opposed to developing cutting-edge technology tools solely for large businesses and wealthy individuals, visionaries must create innovative tools and resources that improve the quality of life for all people. While it is great that SpaceX successfully sent astronauts and private citizens into space and Captain Kirk got the thrill of a lifetime, at least 21 million and as many as 162 million Americans remain unconnected to the internet.[99] On the other hand, the partnership between Columbia University and Stanford University uses virtual reality (VR) to provide individuals with an immersive experience that allows them to walk in the shoes of a Black male in America.[100] Those are the kind of breakthroughs that will benefit us all. Americans have the intelligence to figure this stuff out—we just have not committed to doing so.

Producers

From small businesses to large corporations, producers in this new model make safe, ethically sourced products. Ideally, they would conform to the B Corporation model using business as a force for good, while meeting verified social and environmental per-formance, public transparency, and legal accountability. B Corps like Patagonia give 100 percent of their profits from Black Friday sales to grassroots nonprofits working to protect air, water, and soil quality. Another B Corp, Bombas, a maker of socks and T-shirts, has donated more than $29 million in clothing items to homeless shelters, courtesy of its "buy one, give one" model. These compa-nies have dedicated themselves to doing well and doing good at the same time.

Contributors

Contributors encompass all citizens. Each of us has value; we just need opportunities to test out how we can maximize our individual contributions. This will require us to recognize and value different definitions of success besides money. As long as money is perceived as the ultimate measure of success, some individuals will adopt the mindset that the end justifies the means.

In a workplace setting, all employees must be respected and treated as someone of value. We should really be talking about employee "contributions" rather than employee "performance." All employees are capable of making meaningful contributions to pursue the vision of an organization and help it achieve its mission.

Adapters

Adapters encompass individuals transitioning between careers, retirees looking to pursue a late-stage career, and gig workers seeking flexible work arrangements. Because people are living longer than ever, we need to rethink our rules and expectations regarding retirement. The average sixty-five-year-old is expected to live another 19.3 years, which is over six years longer than it was in 1940. Moreover, seven out of ten people now want to have some sort of work during retirement.[101] Some of them will be giggers. The gig economy is fast expanding, expected to increase from 57.3 million gig workers in 2017 to 86.5 million in 2027.[102] And in 2019, the AARP predicted a "historic surge" in workers above the age of sixty-five in coming decades.[103]

Traditionalists

Traditionalists, rather than trying to cling to the status quo as they do today, must work to keep a society or company grounded in its expressed core values. Traditionalists can be proponents of innovation, but such people must hold leaders accountable for their actions to maintain a safe and equitable workplace and pursue business practices that do not harm people or the planet.

For this new system to work, individuals must understand and put aside our inferior evolutionary traits, avoiding the traps that have resulted in humanity's problems. We need to take advantage of the human intellect to encourage positive behaviors for all humankind. Here are a few ways to tap the power of our big brains.

THE COMMON-SENSE FALLACY

In today's divided, politically charged atmosphere, critical thinking is in short supply. We rely on what we believe to be common sense to quickly draw conclusions and make decisions involving complex subjects. The problem is that we trade accuracy for efficiency and fail to see the layers of complexity associated with particular challenges. For example, some individuals believe if the weather is unseasonably cold on a particular day, common sense suggests global warming is just a hoax. I call this the Common-Sense Fallacy.

Such facile determinations can have profound consequences. For example, if it's suggested there are more open jobs than available workers, common sense leads us to draw a conclusion that unemployed people must be lazy or lack the initiative to work. If kale is really healthy, then just eating kale all of the time will make them healthy. If the police brutalize someone, they did so in defense. When business taxes are reduced, common sense implies the savings will be used to hire more workers.

Obviously, what we know as common sense is exceptionally unreliable as a decision-making tool, as it overlooks fact-based science, history, and other analytical conclusions and contexts. It's merely a simple way to narrow the options and make a fast decision. It's a far cry from what I describe as Level Three Thinking—the application of knowledge, facts, and techniques to sift through other possible answers to a question before drawing conclusions. It requires asking the question "why" at least three times before drawing conclusions.

CONFIRMATION BIAS

Another common logic flaw is confirmation basis, whereby people have programmed themselves to see what they expect, want, or need to see, as opposed to accepting reality and truth.

An example is a math teacher who frequently calls on boys for answers in class because of the widespread and erroneous perception that girls are not as biologically qualified to correctly answer a math question. Another is the fact that teachers send Black boys to detention at roughly three times the rate for the same infractions committed by White boys, since Black boys are considered to act up more often than White boys.[104]

In medicine, doctors perform unnecessary surgeries because of confirmation bias. In the criminal justice system, confirmation bias affects who gets arrested, whether they're convicted, and the length of their sentence. Prisoners are sentenced to death because evidence is interpreted using this logic flaw. In workplaces, predetermined beliefs affect who is hired, how people are evaluated, how they are paid, who gets promoted, and how employees are disciplined.

Confirmation bias is more complex than merely having the certainty that one is correct in their determinations and actions. When processing information supporting our beliefs (even when these viewpoints are incorrect), people experience a rush of dopamine, producing an addictive high. In other words, the decisions generated through this logic flaw strengthen and justify the original confirmation bias.

INFORMATION OVERLOAD

Human beings have access to more information today than at any other point in history. In fact, 90 percent of the data available in 2019 was created in the previous two years.[105] Approximately 1.5 billion people are active on Facebook each day and more than 4 million YouTube videos are watched per minute.[106] Anyone with a working smartphone can access hundreds of cable, satellite, or streaming channels and satellite radio stations.

Yet more is not necessarily better. Human beings can only process a certain amount of information at any given time, resulting in information overload, at a cost to the US economy of nearly $1 trillion a year.[107] Has all this information made us smarter as a species? Not necessarily, according to a study by the University of London, suggesting the distractions caused by a constant barrage of information and notifications reduces IQ by nearly ten points.[108]

Paradoxically, the abundance of information actually makes it more difficult to be well informed, according to 58 percent of respondents to a survey by the Gallup/Knight Foundation.[109] People either shut down completely or turn exclusively to sources they trust, which only tell them what they want to hear, confirming their existing biases.

The balanced reporting on the nightly network news has lost a significant portion of its audience. According to the Edelman Trust Barometer,[110] only 51 percent of people trust the news media. This mistrust is particularly strong among Republicans—67 percent believe the bias in news reporting makes it difficult to sort out facts, compared to 26 percent of Democrats.[111]

Former US President Donald Trump's message that the news media was the enemy of the people especially resonated with his older constituents, a group particularly vulnerable to misinformation. Age is a significant predictor of one's ability to distinguish fact from fiction, according to a study conducted by the Pew Research Center and summarized here.[112]

Age	All 5 Factual Statements as Factual	All 5 Opinion Statements as Opinion
18-29	34%	46%
30-49	30%	42%
50-64	22%	29%
65+	17%	21%

% of U.S. adults in each age group who correctly classified statements as fact or opinion.

In the study, individuals were asked to identify whether a series of statements were factual or based on opinion. The fact that so many adults struggle to discern accuracy from fabrication regarding crucial information is troubling, particularly if one's goal is to reason with people and inspire them to change their viewpoints. We are living in an era of constant and repetitive falsehoods, where free speech covenants protected by the Constitution are being used to promote the most outlandish conspiracy theories and outright lies.

THE RISE OF FAKE NEWS

Fake news gets much of its strength from confirmation bias. Again, we see what we want to see. The objectives of people who promote misinformation is to take advantage of existing biases. When Russia disseminated fake news to affect the outcome of the 2016 United States presidential election, they simply capitalized on existing tensions in the US involving race, religion, and immigration.

Sensationalizing rare instances of violence by Mexican immigrants or inventing outright lies like a caravan of Central Americans coming to the US as an "invasion" force confirmed some people's beliefs about criminality within these groups, fueling a rage they believed was justifiable. That rage has been exacerbated by people fearing *White Replacement Theory*, an old idea that has gotten new life on conservative media.

In a similar vein, White domestic terrorists posed as members of Black Lives Matter to write inflammatory blogs and incendiary quotes about White people and generated the predictable result of some people labeling Black Lives Matter a hate group. Such actions succeeded by taking advantage of the underlying resentments that already existed among some White people.

The prevalence of fake news is damaging to the public dialogue, commodifying and often nullifying expertise. Social media has given rise to a network of influencers who are paid by advertisers to weigh in on a host of topics. Sometimes influencers are true experts in their field—educated, trained, and experienced. Other times, they are just gifted at making persuasive arguments, regardless of education, training, or experience.

A simple web search on a particular topic will turn up an array of articles and blogs. Among the top entries might be pieces written by experts and other pieces authored by very persuasive people with little to no expertise. Few people weigh the background or experience of the authors, accepting that both types of writers have valid viewpoints. Whichever writers coincides with the reader's existing beliefs is most likely the one they trust to be telling the truth. The others are merely offering an alternative opinion equating to fake news.

A particularly alarming aspect of fake news is when it takes the form of sensationalist entertainment and becomes more attractive than the real news. Whether it is from the political left or right, fake news draws people in because it appeals to them on an emotional level. Purveyors of fake news test and respond to the intensity by which people consume the information they share. These puppeteers rely on the fact that emotions cloud people's thinking and influence their behavior.

Unsecured Anchoring

Creators and curators of fake news try to reach their targets early and often. Speed is essential because of another logic flaw, anchoring. Consciously and subconsciously, we add excessive value to the first information presented to us. The classic example of anchoring is in negotiations, such as purchasing a car. The salesman's first price suggestion is the artificial focal point, or anchor. Consequently, any price under the anchor feels like a good deal, even if the price is higher than the car is worth.

Politicians are particularly adept at anchoring. If a president argues vigorously that the public confronts a threat level of 10 on a scale of 1 to 10, then later maintains that through their efforts the threat level has been reduced to 7, we are relieved and supportive, even if a threat level of 5 is usually enough to concern us.

Anchoring is also evident in life experiences that make an indelible mark. For example, parents are likely to raise their children the way they were raised (the anchor), even if research suggests they should do things differently. From a diversity perspective, early impressions matter. If parents are racist, sexist, homophobic, xeno-phobic, or just mean-spirited, these tendencies are anchors for their children, making it difficult for them to engage in interactions with groups of people outside their experience and comfort zone. The good news is that anchoring also serves to cultivate more positive behaviors, assuming parents are mindful of the lasting impact of their early interactions with their children.

THE DUNNING-KRUGER EFFECT

One of the most insidious cognitive biases occurs when people believe they know more about a complex matter than they actually do, a condition known as the Dunning-Kruger effect.

In an article in the *Journal of Personality and Social Psychology*, social psychologists David Dunning and Justin Kruger introduced research indicating that participants who score in the bottom 25 percent on tests of humor, grammar, and logic significantly over-estimate their test performance and ability.[113] They are unable to distinguish the difference between poor and good performance—in other words, they don't know enough to know that they don't know enough. Yet they are more confident in their "knowledge" than actual subject-matter experts, who know enough about a subject to know that they don't know everything. An example is Robert F. Kennedy Jr., formerly a self-proclaimed environmentalist who has now remade himself as a self-proclaimed expert on the evils of vaccinations, to the chagrin of his siblings.[114]

To determine how overconfident people can be, Yale University psychologist Leonid Rozenblit set up an experiment where he asked study participants to rate their knowledge on how ordinary things, such as a refrigerator, work. The participants verbally expressed that they had high levels of knowledge. Yet when asked to explain exactly how things work, their confidence level dropped significantly.[115] This phenomenon is called the illusion of explanatory depth.

The takeaway from this can help us when confronted with an individual with strong opinions about complex subjects like poverty, healthcare, immigration, taxes, or government spending. Calmly ask them to explain in detail how they came to their conclusions. Did this understanding derive from a homemade YouTube video espousing a particular conspiracy theory, or was it absorbed after hearing a self-proclaimed "expert" who lacked specific credentials to comment on the subject?

If this is the case, patiently explain that the information provider is not a reliable source and advise the listener to do the research needed to acquire the viewpoints of bona fide experts. When people realize they don't know as much as they thought they did, it can guide them to express more moderate views.

THE FAILURE OF EDUCATION

The keys to avoiding these common traps are to know they exist and possess the skills to work through them. Unfortunately, the K–12 public school system in the US has failed to offer vital instruction.

Nearly thirty years have passed since the publication of "A Nation at Risk," the landmark report warning about America's failing school system.[116] Despite spending 35 percent more per student than the average expenditure reported by the National Center for Education Statistics,[117] American students still struggle. In the Organisation for Economic Co-operation and Development's most recent international triennial survey of the knowledge and skills of fifteen-year-olds, the US ranked thirteenth in reading, eighteenth in science, and thirty-seventh in math out of seventy-nine countries.[118]

What these scores don't reveal is infinitely more troubling: students aren't learning critical thinking skills important in everyday life. This causes people to default to the Common-Sense Fallacy, profoundly affecting how each of us sees the world and makes decisions.

The fissures in our information-processing systems threaten not only our way of life but our very lives. This risk is evident in the scores of viral videos showing adults behaving badly toward each other in episodes of road rage, school board conflicts, confrontations at sporting events, political discussions gone wild, and hateful incidents inspired by bias and bigotry.

The latter includes the so-called "Karen" social media phenomenon, the name given to White women who call the police on Black people simply for being Black. Nonthreatening behaviors like entering one's own house in an upscale neighborhood, falling asleep in the laundry room of a college dormitory, bird-watching in Central Park, walking through a New York City hotel where one is staying, or painting *Black Lives Matter* on the driveway of one's own property is cause for some White people to perceive a threat where none exists.

You might imagine social stigma would dissuade individuals from causing these dustups, but it seems each incident sparks another. Behavioral contagion might explain some of these copy-cat spectacles. The aforementioned Dr. Frank writes about behavioral contagion in his latest book, *Under the Influence*.[119] He offers cigarette smoking as an example of something that is harmful but draws in others who want to emulate the smoker.

Understanding and avoiding the logic and behavioral traps contributing to bigotry is key for humanity to achieve a consensus on our collective problems to formulate reasonable solutions. This process begins with a comprehensive review and radical transformation of the K–12 public education system, building a sustainable model positioning all students to thrive.

The alternative is to stick with an outdated system of public education designed in the mid-1600s to teach Anglo-Saxon Protestant values. Puritans taught reading so children could study the Christian Bible, but made no attempt to teach subjects like math and science. Schools reinforced socioeconomic inequalities. Girls, for instance, were allowed to attend but taught only to read and not write. Black people held in bondage were taught nothing and forbidden to read and write.

White males had the upper hand educationally for centuries to come. With the onset of the Industrial Revolution in the mid-1700s, White boys were taught math and science. In the mid-1800s, private preparatory schools were established in the Northeast to feed the male children of wealthier families into the Ivy League, the nation's earliest colleges. The Bureau of Indian Affairs developed boarding schools to "civilize" (or "whiten") Indigenous people. The purpose was to "kill the Indian, save the man," according to Brigadier General Richard Henry Pratt, the long-standing headmaster of the most infamous of these schools, the Carlisle Indian School, in Carlisle, Pennsylvania.[120]

During Reconstruction, tax-funded public schools for White people were established, yet newly freed Black people had to develop their own schools with no government assistance. Finding qualified Black teachers was a challenge in the South, as few Black adults could read or write due to these prohibitions. Teachers were recruited from the North to fill the gap. Schools remained segregated until 1954, when the Supreme Court in *Brown v. Board of Education* declared that separate was "inherently unequal."

Nearly seventy years after *Brown*, most American schools remain segregated. Only 12.9 percent of White students attend a school where the majority of students are non-White, while 69.2 percent of Black students attend schools where the majority of students are White.[121] Schools also remain unequal in terms of funding. School districts where the majority of students are White receive over $23 billion more in funding than districts where the majority of students are non-White. Even poor school districts in predominantly White neighborhoods receive an average of 11 percent more in funding than poor non-White school districts.[122]

Other inequities abound. A textbook taught in one state will often differ from the same title in other states, with depictions of key elements of American history altered to reflect a state's political ideology, according to the book, *Lies My Teacher Told Me: Everything*

Your American History Textbook Got Wrong, by James W. Loewen, professor emeritus of sociology at the University of Vermont.[123]

Students reading the same published textbook in Alabama and California are reading subtly different versions of important historical events. This is especially the case with regard to teachings on early Americans, the Founding Fathers, and the treatment of Indigenous people, Black people, and the ethnic groups immigrating to the US in search of the American Dream, but truth is not elastic. Propaganda must yield to historical facts for every student across the country to understand why some people remain second-class citizens.

A shift must be made to a real-world curriculum. Technical areas like math and science are important, but they need to be reexamined to ensure they are taught in ways that approximate what really happens at home and on the job. This approach is already being used in higher education. While I was at Cornell University working on my master's degree in Industrial & Labor Relations, several classmates took the opportunity to enroll in an immersion program. Rather than sitting in a traditional classroom, they took field trips to businesses and spoke directly to their leaders. The projects were cross-functional, with portions of each discipline—labor relations, compensation and benefits, recruiting and staffing, etc.—embedded into them. Without this real-world context, the lackluster outcomes of our public schools suggest not all kids will find the concepts interesting or of use.

A real-world curriculum also needs to encompass the fact that we are all connected. For example, the financial markets in different countries are interconnected, the upheaval in one economy affecting the stability of others. Similarly, poor environmental practices in one country compounds the world's environmental degradation. And borders were obviously of little consequence in stopping the spread of COVID-19.

Historically, global interconnectedness was the accepted wisdom, but it has given way recently to nationalist tendencies. It is not far-fetched to think that textbooks in certain states are being rewritten to downplay the importance of globalization, whipping up fears of supposed foreign aggressors, among them historic allies. Students may come away thinking our allies are our enemies.

What if students instead collaborated with their global peers to complete assignments together over the internet? What if every student in the US graduated high school with fluency in English and another language (or two)? What if study-abroad opportunities were available to every student and not just children whose families can afford them?

In an increasingly diverse world, emphasis needs to be placed on understanding and embracing diversity, equity, inclusion, and belonging. The greatest way to achieve this aim is by experiencing other cultures and unique and different perspectives. This is no longer a nice-to-have; it's a must. How can children advance in an increasingly diverse workplace without demonstrating they are eager to connect with people from different backgrounds? The answer is clear—they can't.

EMOTIONAL INTELLIGENCE

At the heart of our capability to connect with each other is emotional intelligence (EI), the ability to understand and manage one's emotions while interpreting and responding to others'. Daniel Goleman popularized EI in his paradigm-shattering 1995 book, *Emotional Intelligence,* which sold more than 5 million copies worldwide.

EI uses psychology and neuroscience to understand our natural vulnerabilities to the influence of emotions. At key decision points, a battle rages in our minds between cognition, the mental process of gaining knowledge and comprehension, and emotion, behaviors reflecting the personal significance of a thing, event, or state of affairs. When emotion overrides thinking, we may fail to consider the impact of our actions and decisions. Emotion can be a bully, steadily poking and prodding cognition into submission.

Examples of this phenomenon are everywhere. Consider the millions of people each year who pledge to exercise and diet to lose weight. The parking lots at local gyms in the first week of January are full; two months later, they're half-empty. Despite promising themselves they will change their eating habits, when presented with poor food options, these "dieters" find their resolve faltering. Office celebrations, birthdays, funerals, dinner with friends, and other special occasions present obstacles many people can't overcome.

Take chocolate cake, the always formidable foe for chocolate-lovers on a diet. Cognition is the angelic mini-them perched on one shoulder saying, "The cake is off limits." Emotion is the devilish mini-them on the other shoulder purring, "Doesn't that cake look and smell delicious?" The little devil eventually wins, and the chocolate-lover eats the cake, feeling guilt and shame after cheating on their diet. To ease the guilt, they rationalize, "I had a great workout today, so I could afford to have a piece of cake," or, "There was a strawberry on the top of the cake, so it wasn't entirely unhealthy."

Positive behavioral modifications require the application of EI in real time, meaning we must become mindful of the battle raging between cognition and emotion. In recognition that our emotions are attempting to influence our behaviors, we have a better chance of making healthier decisions. EI is also useful when interacting with people holding different perspectives. Pause and consider: How do I feel? Where does that feeling come from? How would I feel if the opposing argument was true? The answers to these questions require impulse control, problem-solving, empathy, and social awareness—all aspects of EI.

To help business leaders learn EI, large companies typically turn to expensive consultants and executive coaches. Wouldn't it be more effective for individuals to develop these skills early, at the K–12 level? Such skills would help students believe in themselves and the value of their contributions. They would learn the importance of empathy while also becoming confident, assertive, and independent, blazing their own trails instead of succumbing to peer pressure. A whole world of possibilities would be there for the taking, despite their different backgrounds and environment.

Investing more K–12 resources into EI also increases the likelihood that students will do better in STEM (science, technology, engineering, and mathematics) subjects. A meta-analysis of 213 evidence-based EI programs involving some 270,000 students suggested that students achieved an 11 percent gain in their academic achievements.[124]

Institutions of higher learning are beginning to accept this value, introducing EI courses across the country. Stanford University is a pioneer, whose leadership has long understood the importance of EI. Nearly every MBA student at Stanford takes Organizational Behavior 374: Interpersonal Dynamics, essentially a class in EI. This course, offered for fifty years at Stanford, is now open to non-students. Yale is on board with the same approach, sponsoring the Center for Emotional Intelligence, teaching children and adults how to develop their own EI. But you don't have to enroll in one of these programs to improve your EI. The first step is practicing emotional self-awareness. Work to become more conscious of your strong feelings and identify your triggers.

Ask yourself the following questions:

- Why do I really feel this way?
- What is the impact of this feeling on my behavior?
  How does this behavior affect me?
- How does this behavior affect others?

Use the answers to those questions to plan and practice the reactions you want to have and the behavior you want to exhibit.

WE MUST DO BETTER

The systemic challenges persisting in America endure because we are human beings, vulnerable to perspectives that produce behaviors affecting the common good. Looking in the mirror and acknowledging our flaws doesn't make us weak; it makes us strong. Challenging bigoted or self-serving policies doesn't make us unpatriotic; it makes us patriots, as we live in a country of free speech and must hold America to its most uplifting ideals.

To create a society that respects and protects vulnerable individuals and communities, all of us—citizens, elected officials, business leaders, policymakers, educators, parents, and nonprofit leaders—must band together. We must do so now, as made even more evident by a string of recent events proving the imprudence of waiting on the next stage of our evolution.

The COVID-19 pandemic; the economic recession it ignited; the unequal imposition of the recession's financial duress on different groups of people; the killing of George Floyd, Breonna Taylor, and other Black people by White police officers; and the siege on the US Capitol by White supremacists and domestic terrorists inspired to act by a president spreading false claims of a stolen election have shown people the world over how challenging life is for their fellow travelers, born on the wrong side of the tracks. We can and must do better.

[93] Juliana Menasce Horowitz, Ruth Igielnik, and Rakesh Kochhar, "Most Americans Say There is Too Much Economic Inequity in the US, but Fewer than Half Call it a Top Priority," *Pew Research Center*, January 9, 2020, https://www.pewresearch.org/social-trends/2020/01/09/trends-in-income-and-wealth-inequality/.

[94] "Distributional Financial Accounts," Federal Reserve Bank of St. Louis, accessed March 19, 2021, https://fred.stlouisfed.org/release?rid=453.

[95] Carmen Ang, "The Rich Got Richer During COVID-19. Here's How American Billionaires Performed," Visual Capitalist, December 30, 2020, https://www.visualcapitalist.com/the-rich-got-richer-during-covid-19-heres-how-american-billionaires-performed/.

[96] Madeline Will, "Which States Have the Highest and Lowest Teacher Salaries?" Education Week, April 30, 2019, https://www.edweek.org/teaching-learning/which-states-have-the-highest-and-lowest-teacher-salaries/2019/04; Carey Ann Nadeau, "New Living Wage Data for Now Available on the Tool," Massachusetts Institute of Technology, May 17, 2020, https://livingwage.mit.edu/articles/61-new-living-wage-data-for-now-available-on-the-tool.

[97] "Childcare Worker Salary," Career Explorer, 2019, https://www.careerexplorer.com/careers/childcare-worker/salary/.

[98] "A Profile of the Working Poor, 2018," US Bureau of Labor Statistics, July 2020, https://www.bls.gov/opub/reports/working-poor/2018/home.htm.

[99] Lexey Swall, "Who's Not Online in America Today?" The Pew Charitable Trusts, May 29, 2020, https://www.pewtrusts.org/en/research-and-analysis/articles/2020/05/29/whos-not-online-in-america-today.

[100] "Empathy and Perspective Taking," Virtual Human Interaction Lab Stanford University, 2020, https://vhil.stanford.edu/projects/2020/empathy-and-perspective-taking/.

[101] Scott Hanson, "Many Americans Don't Enjoy Retirement," Kiplinger, March 30, 2017, https://www.kiplinger.com/article/retirement/t012-c032-s014-many-americans-don-t-enjoy-retirement.html.

[102] Maciej Duszyński, "Gig Economy: Definition, Statistics & Trends [2021 Update]," Zety, February 19, 2021, https://zety.com/blog/gig-economy-statistics.

[103] Kenneth Terrell, "Who's Working More? People Age 65 and Older," AARP, November 22, 2019, https://www.aarp.org/work/working-at-50-plus/info-2019/surging-older-workforce.html.

[104] "2015–16 Civil Rights Data Collection: School Climate and Safety," US Department of Education, Office for Civil Rights, 2018, https://www2.ed.gov/about/offices/list/ocr/docs/school-climate-and-safety.pdf.

[105] Bernard Marr, "How Much Data Do We Create Every Day? The Mind-Blowing Stats Everyone Should Read," *Forbes*, May 21, 2018, https://www.forbes.com/sites/bernardmarr/2018/05/21/how-much-data-do-we-create-every-day-the-mind-blowing-stats-everyone-should-read/#10c9c24b60ba.

[106] Ibid.

[107] Ibid.

[108] Will Knight, "'Info-Mania' Dents IQ More than Marijuana," New Scientist, April 22, 2005, https://www.newscientist.com/article/dn7298-info-mania-dents-iq-more-than-marijuana/.

[109] Jeffery M. Jones and Zacc Ritter, "Americans Struggle to Navigate the Modern Media Landscape," *Gallup*, January 23, 2018, https://news.gallup.com/poll/226157/americans-struggle-navigate-modern-media-landscape.aspx.

[110] "Edelman Trust Barometer 2021," Edelman, 2021, https://www.edelman.com/sites/g/files/aatuss191/files/2021-03/2021%20Edelman%20Trust%20Barometer.pdf.

[111] Jones, Ritter, "Americans Struggle to Navigate."

[112] Jeffery Gottfried and Elizabeth Grieco, "Younger Americans are Better than Older Americans at Telling Factual News Statements from Opinions," Pew Research Center, October 23, 2018, https://www.pewresearch.org/fact-tank/2018/10/23/younger-americans-are-better-than-older-americans-at-telling-factual-news-statements-from-opinions/.

[113] Justin Kruger and David Dunning (1999), "Unskilled and Unaware of It: How Difficulties in Recognizing One's Own Incompetence Lead to Inflated Self-assessments," *Journal of Personality and Social Psychology*, 77(6), 1132, https://doi.org/10.1037/0022-3514.77.6.1121.

[114] Katherine Kennedy Townsend, Joseph P. Kennedy II, and Maeve Kennedy McKean, "RFK Jr. Is Our Brother and Uncle. He's Tragically Wrong About Vaccines," *POLITICO Magazine*, May 8, 2019, https://www.politico.com/magazine/story/2019/05/08/robert-kennedy-jr-measles-vaccines-226798/.

[115] Leonid Rozenblit and Frank Keil (2010), "The Misunderstood Limits of Folk Science: an Illusion of Explanatory Depth," *Cognitive Science*, 26(5), 542, https://doi.org/10.1207/s15516709cog2605_1.

[116] The National Commission on Excellence in Education, "A Nation at Risk: The Imperative of Educational Reform," US Department of Education, April, 1983, https://edreform.com/wp-content/uploads/2013/02/A_Nation_At_Risk_1983.pdf.

[117] "Education Expenditures by Country," The National Center for Education Statistics (NCES), accessed May, 2020, https://nces.ed.gov/programs/coe/indicator_cmd.asp.

[118] "PISA 2018 Results," Programme for International Student Assessment (PISA), accessed January 25, 2022, https://www.oecd.org/pisa/publications/pisa-2018-results.htm.

[119] Robert H. Frank, *Under the Influence: Pitting Peer Pressure to Work* (Princeton: Princeton University Press, 2020).

[120] "'Kill the Indian, and Save the Man': Capt. Richard H. Pratt on the Education of Native Americans," Carlisle Indian School Digital Resource Center, accessed January 25, 2022 http://carlisleindian.dickinson.edu/teach/kill-indian-and-save-man-capt-richard-h-pratt-education-native-americans.

[121] Emma García, "Schools are Still Segregated, and Black Children are Paying a Price," Economic Policy Institute, February 12, 2020, https://www.epi.org/publication/schools-are-still-segregated-and-Black-children-are-paying-a-price/.

[122] Lauren Camera, "White Students Get More K–12 Funding Than Students of Color: Report," US News, February 26, 2019, https://www.usnews.com/news/education-news/articles/2019-02-26/white-students-get-more-k-12-funding-than-students-of-color-report.

[123] James W. Loewen, *Lies My Teacher Told Me: Everything Your American History Textbook Got Wrong* (New York City: Touchstone, 2007).

[124] "Fundamentals of SEL," CASEL, accessed January 25, 2022, https://casel.org/what-is-sel/.

CHAPTER 5

THE EVOLVING ROLE
OF AMERICAN
BUSINESS

The relationship between business and government is built on a simple premise—companies make things, provide services, and hire people, passing on a percentage of their revenues and profits as taxes to federal, state, and local governments, while also contributing to the growth of GDP, an indicator of general economic health. Policymakers track GDP when developing responsive government programs and public policies.[125]

This symbiosis is predicated on a theoretical principle: when companies do well, the nation—the community of people living in a physical territory—prospers. The problem is that not everyone prospers equally as a nation prospers, particularly Black people living in disadvantaged areas with poor healthcare, substandard schools, and few well-paying jobs within the physical territory.

One hundred eighty-one CEO members of the esteemed Business Roundtable set about to change the status quo on August 19, 2019. The CEOs issued a new statement on the purpose of a corporation. Rather than prioritizing profit and the interests of shareholders and other investors as the long-understood business purpose of a corporation, the CEOs adopted a broader purpose, which they referred to as "a stakeholder responsibility."

Who are these additional stakeholders? They include customers, employees, contractors, and the communities in which corporations operate.[126] The surprise announcement aligned with the findings of a societal impact survey by consulting firm Deloitte,[127] which suggested that 93 percent of business leaders believe companies are more than just employers—they are also stewards of society.

This enlightened sense of corporate social responsibility (CSR) is to be lauded, but it is table stakes. Actions speak louder than words. Many of the CEOs in the Business Roundtable were both mum and inactive as protests across the country erupted over systemic racism. Several issued blanket statements deploring violence. Few took a more significant stand; most were fearful their words and actions might compel certain groups of customers to take their business elsewhere.

Others went out on a limb, such as Chobani, a maker of yogurt. As federal and state governments fight about increasing the minimum wage to $15 per hour, Chobani's founder and CEO Hamdi Ulukaya has already paid that minimum wage to employees, 30 percent of who are immigrants and refugees. "We as companies have responsibilities to do these things; we cannot let the government decide," Ulukaya said. "Your responsibilities are not only to make money for your shareholders, but (for) all stakeholders."[128]

There is a term describing such socially responsible corporate actions: conscious capitalism, the belief that businesses must operate ethically and with a higher purpose as they pursue profits, serving both humanity and the environment. Chobani reflects conscious capitalism in all decisions, partnering with food banks, for example, to ensure schoolchildren in disadvantaged neighborhoods do not go hungry.

Other companies have hinged their future profits to similar efforts. Dan Price, CEO of Gravity Payments, for example, stunned his 120 employees in 2015 when he increased their salaries to at least $70,000, effectively doubling some salaries. To accommodate the capital outlay, Price slashed his $1 million salary by 90 percent. Not only did he dramatically change some employees' lives, but the company increased its market share.[129]

In 2020, as the pandemic raged, Gravity Payment's employees returned the gesture, volunteering to give up part of their salaries to ensure everyone remained employed. Some gave back their entire salary. Again, these noble actions paid off, helping the company expand its business during the recession. There is undeniable economic value in doing well by doing good.

Lego's impressive commitment to sustainability also must be mentioned. The air we breathe and the products we use are composed of chemicals linked to health problems. Previous government efforts to regulate industrial behaviors were marginalized during the Trump Administration, on the grounds that the environmental standards were costly and uncompetitive. Lego did its own thing, committing to using environmentally friendly materials in making its core products by 2030.

Corporate leadership is also evident in the Pledge 1% campaign, where Salesforce encourages other companies to join to give 1 percent of equity, 1 percent of time, 1 percent of product, and/or 1 percent of profits to support community nonprofits. The company has given away well over $240 million in grants, provided product donations to more than 39,000 nonprofits and education institutions, and tallied some 3.5 million hours of community service.[130]

Conscious capitalism also is evident in the organization OneTen, which comprises companies across diverse industries committed to hiring, upskilling, and promoting Black people into family-sustaining careers. Companies committing to OneTen's purpose include IBM, Merck, Verizon, Walmart, and Bank of America, among more than a dozen others. Launched in 2020, OneTen's goals include connecting Black people without college degrees with employers offering careers with advancement opportunities and greater economic mobility.

Certainly, the many B Corps formed over the past decade to leverage business as a force for good provide growing evidence that conscious capitalism is smart capitalism. B Corps are for-profit businesses graded by the nonprofit B Lab as meeting the highest standards of social and environmental performance and legal accountability to act with integrity and public transparency. Companies like Patagonia, Bombas, Eileen Fisher, and Stonyfield Farm number among these enlightened organizations in the emerging economy, which commit to the following standards:

- That we must be the change we seek in the world.
- That all business ought to be conducted as if people and place matters.
- That, through their products, practices, and profits, businesses should aspire to do no harm and benefit all.
- To do so requires we act with the understanding that we are each dependent upon another and thus responsible for each other and future generations.

Ben & Jerry's, another B Corp, whose corporate statements condemning racial inequity frequently go viral, lives by these pledges. When former NFL quarterback Colin Kaepernick lost his position for kneeling during the playing of the National Anthem, Ben & Jerry's named a flavor after him—"Change the Whirled" vegan ice cream. The company created the flavor to celebrate "Kaepernick's courageous work to confront systemic oppression and to stop police violence against Black and Brown people."[131]

Other large corporations are making a difference. Lowe's has partnered with Daymond John, star of the TV show *Shark Tank*, to give hundreds of minority-owned small businesses the opportunity to break through traditional impediments to pitch their products to a Fortune 50 retailer. I had the opportunity to meet John when

I interviewed him about his tips for success for a webcast at UKG. Where others see walls, he sees a ladder.

The shift toward a financial system that works for everyone is long overdue. The profit-driven approach to increasing shareholder value serves only those people with the financial means to invest in stocks, which explains why upper-income families now have more than seven times as much wealth as middle-income families and seventy-five times as much as lower-income families.[132] Some of these very shareholders are applying their own pressure on corporations to develop a broader perspective. Socially-conscious investors have developed a set of criteria to screen potential investments that address environmental, social, and governance (ESG) concerns.

The revolutionary idea of companies running businesses with purpose-driven goals beyond profits requires actions both inside and outside the organization. Solving diversity problems within the walls of an organizations is important, but many Black employees still have to drive back to segregated neighborhoods, where they are at high risk of being pulled over by the police on the way. This racial profiling is endemic, with Black people suspected of shoplifting at retail stores, charged higher interest rates for home loans, treated differently at the doctor's office, or having police called on them just for being Black. Across America are winners and losers, oddly dependent in many cases on the ZIP codes where they live.

There is reason for optimism. Deloitte's 2020 Global Millennium Survey suggests both millennials and generation Z members are resolved to drive positive change in their communities and around the world, insisting that governments and businesses mirror their commitment to society—"putting people ahead of profits and prioritizing environmental stability."[133]

HR IS IN THE DRIVER'S SEAT

As more organizations transition from shareholder value companies to stakeholder value companies, their most important stakeholders are the people they employ. Throughout 2020 and 2021, employees coped with the new work paradigms brought about by the pandemic, in addition to unprecedented health and financial stressors.

If employees are an organization's lifeblood, HR is the heartbeat. Unlike other functional leaders focused on the financial, technical, or operational aspects of the business, HR leaders are uniquely positioned to understand human behaviors, motivations, hopes, and fears to help drive those other areas. Only they can ensure the organization meets its employees' needs, empowering them to thrive professionally and personally.

As businesses take ownership of social, economic, diversity, and equality issues affecting their customers and the people and small businesses in the communities where they operate, HR can be equally instrumental, serving as the eyes, ears, and even the conscience of the company.

Organizations leaned heavily on HR during the pandemic. The function became essential in the early stages as employee safety and health concerns were paramount and work shifted to remote and virtual forms. HR's successes in these areas suggest it can demonstrably lead companies in their pursuit of conscious capitalism. And it must. Three in five HR executives predict HR will rapidly become irrelevant if it doesn't modernize its approach.

The transformation of HR is not something new. Over decades, its function has inched ever closer toward a position of successful people management, guiding efforts to improve work efficiency, productivity, engagement, and inclusion. Historically, however (to paraphrase the late stand-up comedian Rodney Dangerfield), HR professionals didn't get any respect from business leaders and other decision-makers. Consequently, many HR professionals themselves had little respect for the position or the work conducted. As a former HR professional, I saw these dynamics play out firsthand.

For most of my twenty-plus years in HR, I heard colleagues complain about not getting a seat at the table—the opportunity to play an active role in the strategic business decisions of their companies. There is certainly some truth to that. Because profit— especially short-term profit—was the primary focus of business leaders, there was little patience for what they perceived as "touchy-feely" HR stuff.

When some HR executives finally received that long-coveted invitation to sit at the table, they failed to make the contributions that would keep them on the VIP list. As a result, more than 80 percent of CEOs and top business leaders believe their company's HR skills—or lack thereof—are a significant issue.[134] Alternatively, some HR leaders are so enamored with the C-Suite, employees don't trust them to advocate for them. The result is HR being perceived as ineffective by both groups. How did we get to this point?

PERSONNEL TO HUMAN RESOURCES:
A BRIEF HISTORY

The idea of a function focused on "human relations" burgeoned in the early nineteenth century. At the time, workers were treated harshly, with scant concern for their personal welfare. No federal laws governed the length of the workday, and a substantial component of the labor force comprised children under the age of sixteen. Visionary social reformers Robert Owen and Charles Babbage set out to change the situation.[135]

Owen spearheaded efforts to reduce the use of child labor and workday hours, ushering in the revolutionary idea that workers needed to be motivated and not threatened to perform work. Babbage, a mechanical engineer, developed a scientific approach to management later adopted and expanded upon by Frederick Taylor, known as "the father of scientific management," in the early 1900s.

Scientific management, characterized by a system of close supervision and piece-rate incentives, gained widespread acceptance in America and throughout Europe. By measuring how long it took for a worker to complete a particular task, labor flows could be adjusted to reduce time and resources. The upside of this approach was greater efficiency and productivity. The downside was that workers were treated like machines, calibrated and optimized to drive greater profits. Workers often rebelled, and strikes were common. To deal with the aftermath of one of the strikes, the National Cash Register Company developed the first known personnel department in 1901.[136]

Five decades later, the human relations movement emerged. Psychologists such as Elton Mayo criticized the scientific management approach, asserting that workers were human beings with specific physical and psychological needs affecting the quality of their performance. Mayo's Hawthorne Study, for instance, focused on how changes in working conditions and work structure positively affected worker productivity. The study also acknowledged the complexity of human behavior at different life stages.

Building upon these research efforts, Abraham Maslow published his hierarchy of needs in 1943, outlining his motivational theory.[137] The groundbreaking work fueled the development of such fields as industrial psychology, organizational psychology, and organizational behavior. Two years later, Cornell University launched the School of Industrial & Labor Relations, the first college in the world to exclusively focus on workplace studies.

In 1948, the American Society for Personnel Administration (today, the Society of Human Resource Management) was established. Early personnel departments focused on administrative tasks and tactical efforts, shifting to compliance issues with the passage of the Equal Pay Act and Civil Rights legislation in the 1960s.

Three decades later, a great deal of discussion was underway about the need for HR to become more business-oriented. In the late 1990s, while completing my graduate studies at Cornell's ILR School, I learned about the work of HR visionary Dave Ulrich, who had recently introduced the term "strategic partner," which became the rallying cry for HR professionals tired of being treated like overpaid administrative assistants.

But as I began my career in HR, the story on the ground was different than what I had been taught in class. Many HR departments were still inundated with administrative work, and some HR staff members were perfectly happy performing those duties. I regularly experienced clashes between professionals trained in HR and others who had gravitated to HR from other departments where, in some cases, they struggled to perform. In effect, they were "hidden" in HR, much like the awkward Toby Flenderson on the hit TV show *The Office*. Overall, the function was still treated as a minor player by both the C-Suite and employees.

More recently, we have seen HR trying to wear so many hats that the function's specific role feels stitched together. This is especially the case in organizations where HR professionals see their role as advocating for employees *and* the business. Vacillating between putting employees first and looking out for the immediate interests of the business at the same time is a prime example of being stuck between a rock and a hard place.[138]

In some cases, HR is responsible for this imbalance. Due to years of downsizing, rightsizing, and belt-tightening in the aftermath of the financial crisis of 2007–08, many employees were treated like interchangeable pieces in an ever-changing puzzle designed to achieve short-term profits. HR professionals were called upon to facilitate these employment actions, making them perceived co-conspirators with business leaders to preserve their bonuses. Many HR professionals also regularly ignored or downplayed employee complaints about abusive leaders or less-than-ideal working conditions. How, then, could an HR professional be trusted as an employee advocate?

At present, HR departments can be described along a continuum—mocked, ignored, and saddled with compliance in some organizations, and perceived as an indispensable partner driving employee performance and business results in others. Across these polarities are a range of HR archetypes.

The Police Officer

The police officer's primary concern is compliance. Such HR professionals are concerned with policies, rules, and maintaining order. While these folks may help a company avoid litigation, they rarely inspire change. People are often on edge around them and find them hard to trust. They tend to drain employee productivity, creativity, and innovation.

The Administrator

Administrators are proud of their ability to manage the tactical aspects of HR, such as report creation, data input, and employee records management. These are the folks most at risk of losing their jobs to automation, and they know it. They are often light on business acumen and have little interest in dealing with overarching business challenges. They are less likely to attend conferences, earn certifications, or stay in tune with broad HR benchmarks and trends.

The Parent

The HR function has tended to attract "mom and dad" types over the years. These are people who care about and connect well with others. They offer advice and counsel based on their own life experiences. They bring in treats on special occasions and do all they can to make employees feel better. Since they tend to rely more on gut instincts and intuition as opposed to insights afforded by data and analytics, they are often slow to adopt new technologies or adapt to changes in process and procedures.

The Philosopher

The philosopher is well read and often highly educated about employment trends. Such individuals view themselves as thought-leaders and influencers. They have big dreams but often endure problems transforming dreams into actionable plans. They sometimes appear idealistic and out of touch with reality. Consequently, they are not taken seriously.

The Business Partner

This persona is in alignment with Ulrich's strategic partner concept. Such individuals demonstrate a working knowledge of their industry and how to drive business results. They are respected by the C-Suite and valued for their ability to be strategic but struggle with the mundane aspects of their jobs. They also have a difficult time gaining the trust and respect of the employees they serve.

TACTICAL VS. STRATEGIC HR ROLES

While the strategic business partner concept has widely been embraced as the right model for HR, three issues stand in the way:

1) HR must perform many important administrative and compliance-related tasks. This work must be done correctly because mistakes can lead to costly litigation. Some people, the Administrators, are drawn to HR specifically for the opportunity to do this type of work. While many of these tasks have been automated at large companies, someone still must manage the automation process. Moreover, few small companies have the resources to invest in automation solutions, requiring continuing manual execution.

2) Many HR professionals lament that they don't have the time to "be strategic" because they are inundated with administrative tasks. For some, the issue really isn't about time—they don't really understand what it means to be strategic. When asked what they would do if the administrative work magically disappeared, they often draw a blank. They know they want to sit at the

grown-ups' table, but they are unsure how to contribute to the discussion.

3) A significant number of HR professionals who understand what it means to be strategic lack the skills to perform in this capacity. In a recent study, only 30 percent of business leaders believe HR has a reputation for sound business decisions.[139] To overcome this challenge, many CEOs are turning to other disciplines to lead HR. In fact, 40 percent of Chief Human Resources Officers (CHROs) now come from outside business units and not the HR department.[140] This statistic doesn't bode well for traditional HR professionals.

For HR to achieve the respect it desires, new policies, practices, and structures must be formulated and codified. This transformation must begin with a name change. "Human resources" implies that a labor pool, like water or other natural resources, is a reservoir business leaders can tap for whatever they need in the name of profits, despite the intellectual and physical talents it comprises. Even the word "department" sounds archaic, advancing the silo mentality permeating many organizations.

Human resources should be renamed the **People Team**. To help facilitate this transition, we must tear down yesteryear's hierarchical organizational structures and build a new model comprised of two teams that keep the needs of employees at the center.

One team, **People Operations**, would house the administrative and compliance work and coordinate the cloud-based automation solutions. The other team, which represent a more significant shift for HR, would be **Human Insights**. The new People Scientists within this unit would have an undergraduate degree in anthropology, psychology, sociology, or behavioral economics, in addition to a graduate degree in HR Management, knowledge of EI, and an exceptional capacity for critical thinking. The team would apply qualitative and quantitative techniques to craft data-driven solutions that maximize employees' personal and professional success.

PEOPLE OPERATIONS

The important gauges of success of this function are data and process automation, efficiency, and accuracy. Professionals in this area are not tasked with delivering the "strategic" expectations of HR. Individuals drawn to this type of work should not have to endure a "bait and switch" and be asked to do something—strategic work—they are not prepared for and don't want to do anyway.

This is an essential group. Keeping the company out of legal or regulatory trouble, getting employees information they need when they need it, and performing important work, such as benefit administration, should be done by folks who are talented and enjoy doing it.

Human Insights

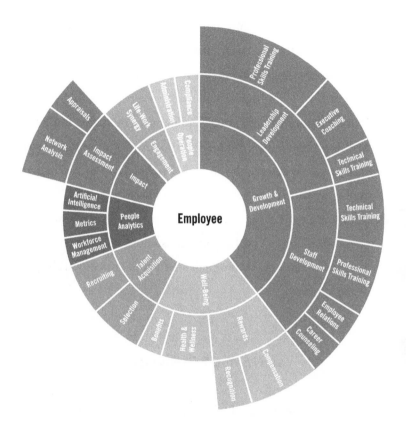

We have to deal with this business partner challenge head-on. HR professionals need to extricate themselves from being hopelessly caught between serving the employees and meeting the demands of business leaders. They need to step back and understand that in this new stakeholder primacy reality, advocating for the employee *is* advocating for the business. If HR overlooks irresponsible, dangerous, or illegal business actions for the short-term benefits of the business, it irrevocably leads to significant long-term issues. Little fires become big ones.

Ignoring employee complaints about an abusive leader, for example, makes the organization vulnerable to lawsuits and reputational damage. Underpaying or overworking talented employees leads to turnover and high replacement costs. Failure to create an inclusive environment for underrepresented employees results in stunted innovation and productivity losses. Eliminating jobs to protect executive compensation and shareholder returns damages the ability to attract and retain talent and hold on to and increase customers and market share. Human Insights professionals work as relationship catalysts, coaches, and consultants and are entrusted with attracting and developing talented people to enjoy fulfilling work and careers.

A NEW BEGINNING

Companies that set the bar high in terms of their stakeholder commitment must be applauded, as they encourage others to follow. Otherwise, they will lose out on the talent needed to lead them into the future and risk alienating customers. Nearly half (47 percent) of millennials, the largest talent pool in the workforce, want CEOs to take a stand on important societal issues. In their employment decisions, 76 percent consider a company's social and environmental commitments, 64 percent won't take a job if a potential employer does not have strong corporate responsibility practices, and 75 percent would take a pay cut to work for a socially responsible company. Moreover, nearly 70 percent actively consider a company's values when making a purchase.[141]

People Teams must not squander the opportunity to reshape their organizations into more purposeful, people-centric operations. As businesses shift from shareholder value to stakeholder value, employees are at the center of this transformation. Transitioning to a people-first philosophy, separating the tactical and strategic elements of the function, renaming aspects of the function away from terms with Industrial Revolution implications, and building robust systems to measure their impact are critical steps in this budding evolution.

It is finally time for the function to transition from Clark Kent to Superman. It is time to take off the glasses. No longer can such important people toil in an unassuming function. The People Team must be bold, fearless, and crystal clear on its priorities, chiefly the need to understand, anticipate, and meet the needs of people, who must be at the center in this shifting paradigm for business from shareholder primacy to stakeholder primacy.

[125] "Measuring a Company's Entire Social and Environmental Impact," B Lab Global, accessed January 25, 2022, https://bcorporation.net/about-b-corps.

[126] "Business Roundtable Redefines the Purpose of a Corporation to Promote 'An Economy That Serves All Americans," Business Roundtable, August 19 2019, https://www.businessroundtable.org/business-roundtable-redefines-the-purpose-of-a-corporation-to-promote-an-economy-that-serves-all-americans.

[127] "The Rise of the Socially Responsible Business," Deloitte, accessed January 25, 2022, https://www2.deloitte.com/global/en/pages/about-deloitte/articles/societal-impact-survey-deloitte-global.html.

[128] Joel Weber, "Chobani's Anti-CEO Is a Pro-Employee Billionaire in Expansion Mode," Bloomberg Businessweek, December 24, 2020, https://www.bloomberg.com/news/features/2020-12-24/chobani-yogurt-ceo-hamdi-ulukaya-is-a-pro-employee-billionaire-in-expansion-mode.

[129] Lauren M. Johnson, "This CEO Raised the Minimum Salary of His Employees to $70k and Now He's Doing It Again," CNN, September 25, 2019, https://edition.cnn.com/2019/09/25/business/gravity-increases-employee-minimum-salary-to-70k-trnd/index.html.

[130] "Pledge 1%," Salesforce.org, accessed January 25, 2022, https://www.salesforce.org/pledge-1/.

[131] Chauncey Alcorn, "Ben & Jerry's Creates Colin Kaepernick–Inspired Vegan Ice Cream Flavor," CNN, December 10, 2020, https://edition.cnn.com/2020/12/10/business/colin-kaepernick-vegan-ice-cream-ben--jerrys/index.html.

[132] Juliana Menasce Horowitz, Ruth Igielnik, and Rakesh Kochhar, "Most Americans Say There is Too Much Economic Inequity in the US, but Fewer than Half Call it a Top Priority," Pew Research Center, January 9, 2020, https://www.pewresearch.org/social-trends/2020/01/09/trends-in-income-and-wealth-inequality/.

[133] "The Deloitte Global Millennial and Gen Z Survey," Deloitte, 2020, https://www2.deloitte.com/global/en/pages/about-deloitte/articles/millennialsurvey.html#.

[134] Arthur H. Mazor, Michael Stephan, Brett Walsh, Hendrik Schmahl, and Jaime Valenzuela, "Reinventing HR," Deloitte Insights, February 27, 2015, https://www2.deloitte.com/us/en/insights/focus/human-capital-trends/2015/reinventing-hr-human-resources-human-capital-trends-2015.html.

[135] Avinash Suresh Meherkar (2018), "Impact of Human Resource Management on Organizational Performance," *International Journal of Current Engineering and Scientific Research (IJCESR)*, 5(5), 110–113, http://troindia.in/journal/ijcesr/vol5iss5part2/110-113.pdf.

[136] Jared Lindzon, "Welcome to the New Era of Human Resources," Fast Company, May 20, 2015, https://www.fastcompany.com/3045829/welcome-to-the-new-era-of-human-resources.

[137] Abraham Maslow, "A Theory of Motivation," *Psychological Review*, 50(4):370–396, 1943, https://doi.org/10.1037/h0054346.

[138] "HR Whitepaper: Reimagining HR for the Augmented Era," Ultimate Software, accessed January 25, 2022, https://www.ultimatesoftware.com/contact/reimagining-hr-for-the-augmented-era.

[139] Arthur H. Mazor, Michael Stephan, Brett Walsh, Hendrik Schmahl, and Jaime Valenzuela, "Reinventing HR," Deloitte Insights, February 27, 2015, https://www2.deloitte.com/us/en/insights/focus/human-capital-trends/2015/reinventing-hr-human-resources-human-capital-trends-2015.html.

[140] Ibid.

[141] "2016 Cone Communications Millennial Employee Engagement Study," Cone Communications, 2017, https://www.conecomm.com/research-blog/2016-millennial-employee-engagement-study.

CHAPTER 6

BUILDING A CULTURE
THAT VALUES DEI&B

"Culture eats strategy for breakfast," management theorist Peter Drucker once said. The challenge for many companies is not formulating a culture but living it. Posting the corporate values and bringing them to life are two different things. People Teams of the future need to lead the charge in building organizational cultures that inspire their employees' loyalty and passion to keep them satisfied and thriving.

According to Glassdoor, culture and values matter most in driving employee satisfaction, followed by senior leadership and career opportunities.[142] The website's study suggests the most important element of culture is demonstrating the value of each person, regardless of background, job title, or job level. For this to occur, the new People Scientists in the Human Insights Team must relate to employees at their level, determining how to keep them engaged in their work and careers *continuously.*

Through employees' work lives, different things will motivate, inspire, frustrate, and anger them. Work and life effectively intertwine into a LifeWork Cluster. This is based on a concept we are exploring at UKG, The LifeWork Journey. The LifeWork Journey evolved from a concept I developed around the Employee Continuum of Needs, which is like Maslow's hierarchy, but the stages are not necessarily sequential. Employees may exhibit combinations of these characteristics at different points in time, moving up and down, depending on events in their lives.

LIFEWORK CLUSTER

At-Risk	Security	Growth	Self-Realization	Influence	Legacy
Feeling vulnerable, such as experiencing financial or health challenges.		Feeling confident and ready to take risks to gain new knowledge, skills, and experiences.		Being motivated to inspire others and help them succeed.	
Feeling safe, personally and professionally.		Enjoying achieving significant personal and professional goals.		Being reflective, seeking to make a lasting impact in chosen areas.	

The boxes transform in size as people move through their journey. For example, at retirement, an employee is likely to be much more concerned with Legacy than Growth, as illustrated here:

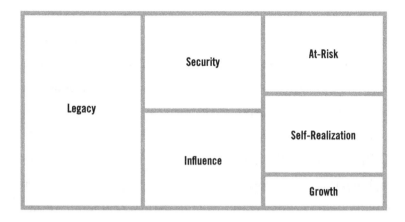

Someone facing a health crisis, on the other hand, will feel At Risk. The person is primarily concerned about their health and possibly their Legacy:

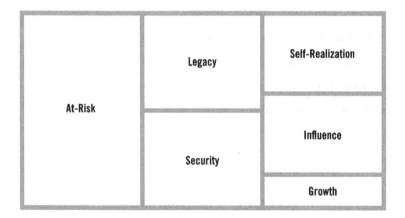

Understanding where someone might fall regarding their LifeWork Cluster can give People Teams insight into how to communicate with them and design programs for them. Technology, in the form of sentiment analysis, natural language processing, and machine learning, can scale the organization's ability to understand its people and create unique experiences for them that will generate high levels of engagement. This is good for the employees as well as the organizations because highly engaged employees outperform their peers by an eye-opening 202 percent.[143]

Thinking about DEI&B (diversity, equity, inclusion, and belonging) in terms of the LifeWork Journey offers a new level of understanding. For example, a diversity initiative may appear threatening to a White male who feels At Risk but may be received as a great opportunity to learn by a White male in Growth mode. A specific company benefit, on the other hand, may appeal to a recent immigrant employee who feels At Risk, living paycheck-to-paycheck, but not to a long-term employee focused on Self-Realization and how they can achieve less immediate goals.

Unless organizations can make significant progress with their diversity efforts, segments of their employee populations will feel disengaged, if not At Risk. This means DEI&B can't be a side initiative; it must be built into every core People Team function in an organization.

TALENT ACQUISITION

While many companies claim diversity is important, employment selection processes have been catastrophic for women and people of color, as well as individuals from other underrepresented groups.

According to US Census data, these groups generally see higher unemployment rates than their male and White counterparts with the same level of education. When these statistics are shared with business leaders, they often respond by saying there is not enough diverse talent out there. This response generates a great deal of emotion from women and people of color because they know many of those organizations simply haven't bothered to look hard enough. For example, if a company is struggling to find women engineers, why wouldn't they recruit at schools with higher numbers of women engineering students? Why not partner with professional associations for women engineers or recruit from all-women's colleges? Likewise, if a company can't find enough Black advertising professionals, why not recruit at historically Black colleges and universities? To get diverse talent, recruiters must go where the diverse populations are.

On the other hand, there is some truth to the notion that there are not enough talented Black people out there. After all, Black people make up only 13 percent of the population, so the simple reality is there are fewer talented Black people when compared to White people because there are fewer Black people when compared to White people—period. Additionally, from birth, many grow up in a system destined to result in them being underrepresented in some areas, such as STEM fields.

Even without any hint of discrimination, it is virtually impossible for a large organization to reflect diversity in their demographic makeup without exercising extraordinary effort. According to Glassdoor, each corporate job opening attracts about 250 applicants.

If the applicant pool composition mirrors the demographics of the US labor pool, 77 percent of applicants would be White (including Hispanic White people), 13 percent Black (including Hispanic Black people), 6 percent Asian, and 4 percent other. That's 193, 33, 15, and 10 applicants, respectively. Of those applicants, only 6 on average are called in for interviews. If we do some rounding, that's 4 White applicants, 1 Black applicant, and 1 Asian applicant, based on their percentages in the population, without any bias in the selection process. The math suggests a successful candidate is four times more likely to be White than Black. How can a company achieve diversity goals under these circumstances? Overcoming this challenge requires recruiters to become intentionally aggressive about overrepresenting Black people in the applicant pools.

Race	Representative Portion of 250	Population Percentage	Representative Portion of 6
White (including White Hispanic)	193	77%	4
Black (including Black Hispanic)	33	13%	1
Asian	15	6%	1
Other	10	4%	0

Once significant numbers of diverse candidates are in the pools, the next challenge is overcoming selection bias. I applaud efforts of companies like my own that provide technologies to discover and remove unconscious bias, but tech alone won't solve our problems.

While bias interrupters and other automated tools can do much of the initial screening, there will continue to be a need for in-person and/or virtual interviews of candidates to discern demonstrated behaviors in alignment with a company's values.

Recruiters also will need to avoid giving too much weight to superfluous job qualifications and inadequately evaluating the actual skills required for the jobs. A candidate with an ability to speak three languages is a gift, but is the person truly right for a job where the likelihood of the third language ever being spoken is slim to none? Regrettably, companies often believe "more is better" and hire accordingly, resulting in the exclusion of underrepresented groups qualified to perform the job and perpetuating workforce homogeneity. More is not always better, particularly if certain skills are not needed.

What Does It Mean to Be Qualified?

Clusters of competencies separate high performers from average performers; unfortunately, these competencies may not be meaningfully assessed in a job interview. As candidates pass through the hiring process, competencies like resilience, determination, political savvy, flexibility, influence, independence, empathy, and self-awareness are discussed at a cursory level, if at all.

Different questions must be asked to generate higher-quality hires. For example, all jobs involve some level of stress, and research indicates these stress levels are getting worse. Shouldn't stress management be an essential qualification for most jobs? Rather than asking candidates if they manage stress well, hiring managers should ask them to provide specific instances when they felt overwhelmed by their workload and how they responded to the pressure.

To understand a candidate's determination to fulfill a job task, interviewers should ask for an example of how they succeeded when the odds were against them. Regardless of the person's background, ask what most separates them from other people. Don't ask them what they would do—ask what they have done and why. The responses will indicate if they truly possess attributes like resilience, determination, flexibility, and so on, making them capable of performing the role better than other candidates. This approach reveals whether or not a candidate's values are aligned with posted corporate values.

A candidate's ability to manage multiple priorities with little direction, deal with rejection, and manage a diverse team is important. Yet these skills and competencies typically take a back seat in the selection process. Someone with great technical skills and test scores who struggles with professional demands is not a highly qualified job candidate.

I listened to Dr. Robert Livingston, lecturer of public policy at Harvard University's John F. Kennedy School of Government, speak about qualifications. He made a compelling case that among the top candidates for jobs, it is virtually impossible to determine who is the most qualified because (1) test scores and GPAs are not a great predictor of job success, so we cannot deem higher scores as evidence of qualifications, and (2) the differences between candidates with the highest cluster of scores is insignificant. In fact, on different days, the test results for those top candidates would vary, with each occupying different positions every day. Based on our current approach, depending on the day, we would deem one more qualified than others.

By broadening the definition of the attributes that make someone qualified, companies are likely to increase workforce diversity *organically*, as opposed to using a targeted strategy that angers overrepresented people and alienates underrepresented people who, others assume, get positions just to meet diversity goals. Think of what this could mean for historically marginalized groups and first-generation college students, people returning to the workforce after raising kids, individuals who've rebounded from trauma, and people from challenging backgrounds who've chosen an atypical life path. The skills they have learned while overcoming life's challenges—adaptability, stress management, optimism, etc.—qualifies them to deal with workplace stressors that could overwhelm others. Certainly, these individuals must meet the minimum technical requirements of the available position, but they should not be overlooked in favor of others with marginally better technical skills that really won't help them perform better on the job.

What About Reverse Discrimination?

If a candidate meets the minimum technical requirements but the hiring focus is on a broader definition of qualifications, no company can be accused of lowering its standards merely to hire people who look different to address the aims of workforce diversity. Organization leaders talk about the importance of diversity, pointing out how different people's unique perspectives on a team combine to increase creativity, innovation, and problem-solving. Yet current hiring processes fail to validate this value. Without this validation, one can hire a woman whose worldview is more closely aligned with males, or a Black person whose worldview has little in common with other Black people. In fact, a male candidate or White candidate with unique life experiences may emerge from the selection process as the more qualified candidate.

Until the right questions are asked of candidates about how their life experiences have prepared them to take on a specific role, companies will be unable to find people whose skills and competencies are optimally aligned with the organization or the job position. For today's People Team and hiring officials to make a significant impact on their organization's diversity, they need to think more deeply about selection criteria. Hiring people with great technical skills is only part of the equation. To be qualified for today's complex, stressful, and demanding workplace, a broader selection of skills and competencies must be part of the equation.

WELL-BEING

One of the most significant opportunities for the new People Teams is to conquer the health and wellness crisis companies are experiencing. Not only are these challenges costly, but they profoundly affect employees, robbing them of the quality of life they could be enjoying. The United States spends more than $3.6 trillion annually on healthcare.[144] The bulk of this expenditure is earmarked to treat chronic health conditions like diabetes, heart disease, and cancer. Obesity, which is a significant risk factor for chronic diseases, now affects nearly 40 percent of the population, with 10 percent of women and 5 percent of men being more than 100 pounds overweight. Consider that companies, on average, spend 42 percent more on healthcare costs for obese employees, compared to employees at a healthy weight.[145]

These numbers are even more disturbing for their Black employees. Over 76 percent of Black adults are overweight or obese compared to 69.8 percent of White adults.[146] Forty-two percent of Black adults suffer from hypertension compared with 28.7 percent of White adults. Black people have the highest mortality rate for all cancers combined compared with any other racial and ethnic group.[147] Overall 13 percent of Black people reported having fair or poor health compared with 8.3 percent of White people.[148] These numbers only got worse during the pandemic, with Black people being three times more likely to be hospitalized and twice as likely to die of COVID-19 compared to White people.[149]

To help employees address these lifestyle challenges, the majority of large firms offer some form of workplace wellness programs, but despite collectively investing more than $8 billion in such programs, the return for companies has been extremely disappointing, with little long-term cost savings or overall improvement in employee health.[150] That's the sobering conclusion of a 2019 Harvard Medical School study published in the *Journal of the American Medical Association* (JAMA). The study found no significant effects on health outcomes like blood pressure, cholesterol, or body mass index. Moreover, there was no decrease in absenteeism, no improvement in job performance, and no reduction in healthcare use or spending.[151] None of this, of course, means company-sponsored wellness programs are completely worthless; many organizations cite isolated employee success stories.

The opportunity to change the healthcare story in America is to identify the mental and emotional challenges holding people back. Employers already pay an estimated $300 billion per year on employees' job-related stress issues.[152] However, these programs don't address major drivers of workplace stress for Black people: individual and structural racism.

Human Insights professionals within the People Teams must begin to offer evidence-based approaches to overcoming these enormous challenges, particularly for individuals from diverse backgrounds who are carrying so much weight—literally and figuratively.

GROWTH AND DEVELOPMENT

People Teams can further drive a culture of belonging by preparing managers to more effectively connect with their employees, which means helping them develop a new set of people-centric skills and competencies. The skills of the future are well-documented:[153]

- Creativity
- Emotional intelligence

- Critical thinking
- Problem-solving
- Active learning with a growth mindset
- Judgment and decision-making
- Interpersonal communication
- Diversity and cultural intelligence
- New technology skills
- Embracing change

While diversity and cultural intelligence is listed as a skill itself, it is really a compilation of the other skills listed. Upskilling and reskilling are high priorities for training departments, 51 percent and 43 percent respectively, but these training programs often fall short because they are usually offered in a lockstep, cookie-cutter approach that fails to meet people where they are.[154] Human Insights professionals need to shift the focus away from these one-size-fits-all training schemes to more customized approaches that offer the right skills at the right time.

LIFEWORK SYNERGY

Another way employees can value their diversity and make people feel more included is to reconsider everything we know about how we work, when we work, and why we work. There is no magic about a forty-hour workweek or an eight-hour workday. Some people are as productive in thirty hours as others are in fifty. Maybe the single greatest learning coming out of the pandemic and the remote work paradigms it spawned is that where a person works or when they work must be based on their own individual circumstances, assuming they can get work done in a timely fashion and don't delay the progress of others.

Holding a single mother with three young kids at home distance learning to the same time commitments as a married empty nester makes little sense. Holding someone who feels they work at peak capacity in the morning to the same schedule as someone whose work capacity peaks at night is bad for them and bad for business. Daniel Pink, author of numerous bestsellers, including his latest, *When: The Scientific Secrets of Perfect Timing*, asserts human beings are best suited to perform different tasks at different times: the morning hours are better suited for analytical tasks, the midday hours are better suited for administrative tasks, and the late afternoon and evening hours are better suited for brainstorming and creative problem-solving. Only a small population of people have different patterns. Why are we not learning about these rhythms and building work around them? (Daniel said he would seek out the Pope to nominate me for sainthood if I could influence my company to create the technology to do just that.)

We must build LifeWork Synergy for our employees. LifeWork Synergy is not about reducing expectations—quite the opposite will occur if people are set up for success on *their* terms and are not held to arbitrary goals targeted for them in some outdated performance management system where people are penalized or rewarded for outcomes beyond their control, via an administratively burdensome process that force-ranks people irrespective of the value of the teams they populate.

Coupling these rankings with compensation is patently unfair, as a manager can "rig the system" when they want to give someone a raise. Members of underrepresented groups are often penalized in this system because they are not part of the good old boy network. The term "performance management" itself is archaic. The word "performance" conjures the image of a show dog trotted out to perform for an audience. We have to demonstrate a higher level of respect for our employees.

Companies need to step back and think about what they are really trying to measure. The goal should be to find ways to get a better handle on each employee's respective contributions, including their accomplishment of quantitative goals in addition to the qualitative value they generate. Today's performance management systems entirely miss situations where the employee has helped others attain their career aspirations, or how collaboratively the employee works with others to get things done, or how the employee represents the organization in the community. The good news is that technology has evolved to determine these attributes. Tools like network analysis can be used to assess and quantify the impact an employee is having on other people. I would propose these discussions go beyond goals and objectives to include discussions about the LifeWork Cluster, as well as what managers can do to help with LifeWork Synergy.

The People Teams of the future will have to do a better job demonstrating their value than legacy HR teams have done. Without the ability to customize and scale their solutions, People Teams will fail to deliver the immense value that is within their potential. Technology is a means to these ends. People Team professionals must embrace automation to make work tasks less manual and burdensome, leverage AI to augment and amplify human capabilities, and use natural language processing (NLP) and sentiment analysis tools that give managers insight into employee emotions. These tools can help People Teams tap into who employees are as individuals—their needs, beliefs, motivations, and decision-making processes.[155] At the core of these processes must be a focus on embracing DEI&B.

[142] Amanda Stansell, "Which Workplace Factors Drive Employee Satisfaction Around the World?" Glassdoor Economic Research, July 11, 2019, https://www.glassdoor.com/research/employee-satisfaction-drivers/.

[143] "State of the Global Workplace," *Gallup*, December, 2017, https://www.gallup.com/workplace/238079/state-global-workplace-2017.aspx?g_source=EMPLOYEE_ENGAGEMENT&g_medium=topic&g_campaign=tiles.

[144] "National Health Expenditure Data," Centers for Medicare & Medicaid Services, accessed December 16, 2020, https://www.cms.gov/Research-Statistics-Data-and-Systems/Statistics-Trends-and-Reports/NationalHealthExpendData/NationalHealthAccountsHistorical.

[145] "Obesity Prevention Source: Economic Costs," Harvard T.H. Chan School of Public Health, April 8, 2016, https://www.hsph.harvard.edu/obesity-prevention-source/obesity-consequences/economic/.

[146] "HUS 2018 Trend Tables," National Center for Health Statistics, 2018, https://www.cdc.gov/nchs/data/hus/2018/026.pdf.

[147] Sofia Carratala and Connor Maxwell, "Health Disparities by Race and Ethnicity," Center for American Progress, May 7, 2020, https://www.americanprogress.org/issues/race/reports/2020/05/07/484742/health-disparities-race-ethnicity/.

[148] "HUS 2018 Trend Tables."

[149] "COVID-19: Hospitalization and Death by Race/Ethnicity," Centers for Disease Control and Prevention, accessed March 21, 2021, https://www.cdc.gov/coronavirus/2019-ncov/covid-data/investigations-discovery/hospitalization-death-by-race-ethnicity.html.

[150] "2018 Employer Health Benefits Survey," Kaiser Family Foundation, October 3, 2018, https://www.kff.org/report-section/2018-employer-health-benefits-survey-section-12-health-and-wellness-programs/.

[151] Zirui Song and Katherine Baicker (2019), "Effect of a Workplace Wellness Program on Employee Health and Economic Outcomes," Journal of the American Medical Association, *321*(15), 1491–1501, https://doi.org/10.1001/jama.2019.3307.

[152] "Financial Costs of Job Stress," University of Massachusetts, accessed January 25, 2022, https://www.uml.edu/research/cph-new/worker/stress-at-work/financial-costs.aspx.

[153] Bernard Marr, "The 10 Vital Skills You Will Need for The Future of Work," *Forbes*, April 29, 2019, https://www.forbes.com/sites/bernardmarr/2019/04/29/the-10-vital-skills-you-will-need-for-the-future-of-work/#54eab0f33f5b.

[154] "2021 Workplace Learning Report: Your Guide to Skill Building in the New World of Work," LinkedIn Learning, accessed January 25, 2022, https://learning.linkedin.com/resources/workplace-learning-report.

[155] Naveen Joshi, "7 Types of Artificial Intelligence," *Forbes*, June 19, 2019, https://www.forbes.com/sites/cognitiveworld/2019/06/19/7-types-of-artificial-intelligence/#2c1b598233ee.

CHAPTER 7

FINDING THE WAY FORWARD

"The government can't do anything right."

"If you really want something done, you should trust a 'bossiness' person to do it."

"Government workers are just lazy."

"The government just wastes money."

"Big government is bad for the economy."

"Government should move out of the way and let the markets take over."

In 2012, I stepped away from my private practice as an executive coach and keynote speaker to run the City of Jacksonville, Florida's HR department. During that time, I was on the receiving end of the above selection of quotes. I was a cog in the spinning wheel of government, with firsthand knowledge of how politicians, appointed officials, and career government employees turned the wheel.

Instead of a pure focus on governing "for the people," many politicians' primary concern is winning the next election. Appointed officials, on the other hand, are typically driven by the rewards they receive for their efforts in helping a politician get elected. And career employees often worry about job preservation and moving up in the governing hierarchy. Like all generalizations, these statements don't acknowledge that there are people in all three governing categories whose public service motivations are pure.

Regarding those outside this cohort of authentic public servants, disorder and confusion are frequent. Many appointed officials have little, if any, experience in the areas they're entrusted to supervise. By the time they master the role, they're replaced by the next elected official. Instead of long-term strategic plans, governmental priorities shift upon the passing of the baton, as campaign contributions and cronyism influence the next administration's direction and the staffing of important positions, resulting in less competent people stumbling around in the years ahead. The same stasis and inertia are evident in Corporate America, where it is often not what you know but *who* you know that gets one hired and promoted.

When citizens complain the government can't get anything done on time or within a budget, they overlook the fact that much of the work is outsourced to the private sector. Roughly 40 percent of the government's discretionary spending goes toward contracts for goods and services.[156] In effect, many failed government projects are managed by private companies. For every $1,000 spent on a toilet seat, a company on the other side of the deal is cashing the check. Certainly, companies bear part of the responsibility for waste and corruption committed by government officials as they are often the instigators and beneficiaries of said waste and corruption.

Yet the political debate is divided along the lines of "big government versus little government." These terms are partisan shorthand to synthesize a message—the size of government is not important. What matters is whether or not government is productive, equitable, efficient, and effective for every citizen and the overall benefit of society. All people must have equal access to a quality education, safe and reliable public transportation, and structurally sound roads and bridges. Similarly, all people should have access to quality healthcare and insurance.

The problem is not higher taxes to support government safety net programs to help people in crisis; the problem is the role of private companies profiting from government contracting. Some private contracts offer perverse incentives for companies to cut costs and maximize profits, to the long-term detriment of citizens.

PRIVATE MATTERS OF PUBLIC CONCERN

A case in point is the government's outsourcing of criminal justice to private prisons whose income depends on putting more people behind bars for as long as possible. Judges Michael Conahan and Mark Ciavarella were sentenced in 2008 to 17.5-year and 28-year prison terms, respectively, for sending young Black kids to privately-run youth centers in exchange for receiving more than $2 million in kickbacks from the company running the centers.[157]

Leaving aside the ethical risks, there is no evidence that private companies are a more cost-effective means of incarceration. According to The Sentencing Project, an organization seeking a fair and effective US criminal justice system, private companies trim prison budgets by employing mostly non-union and low-skilled workers at lower salaries and limited benefits, compared to staff at publicly run institutions. Yet these labor cost savings do not translate into overall cost savings, studies suggest.[158]

Moreover, the outcomes can be catastrophic. At East Mississippi Correctional Facility, charges of unchecked violence, alarming suicide rates, and overall neglect garnered national attention. Called as an expert witness for Mississippi inmates in a federal civil rights lawsuit, Eldon Vail, the former state prisons chief in Washington State, told the court that the focus on cutting costs had sent East Mississippi into a downward spiral.

The role of private companies in our electoral process is equally dubious and destructive. Former Vice President Dick Cheney, for example, received a $34 million severance package after leaving oil and gas company Halliburton to become vice president.[159] During the subsequent Iraq war, a lucrative no-bid contract was awarded to Kellogg, Brown, and Root (KBR), a subsidiary of Halliburton. A whistleblower complaint concerning the nature of the contract award process resulted in a decision by the Defense Contract Audit Agency to hold back more than $553 million in payments for disallowable charges.

Dick Cheney's situation is not isolated. In the Trump administration, former Chief Economic Adviser Gary Cohn received a $285 million package from Goldman Sachs *after* he left to join the administration.[160] Former Secretary of State Rex Tillerson received $180 million upon his departure from Exxon, and former Treasury Secretary Steven Mnuchin received a severance package of almost $11 million when he left CIT Group.[161] Is it farfetched to presume their former employers might have some weight in their governing decisions? Can the public trust their decisions were not bought in advance?

Money "talks," as is often said. The candidate with the biggest financial war chest wins most of the time. This was true in 2016 for about 95 percent of candidates seeking to win or preserve House seats and for approximately 85 percent of candidates seeking to win or preserve Senate seats. According to OpenSecrets.org, candidates for federal and state races spent a whopping $6.5 billion, an obscene amount considering the issues with poverty, hunger, and homelessness in America.[162]

In 2020, spending was even more alarming. Joe Biden raised more money in a month than Donald Trump did over the entirety of his 2016 run. In Congressional races, the candidate with the most cash won more than 88 percent of the time.[163] The year 2020 goes down in history as the most expensive election ever, and that spending included at least $100 million in "dark money," funds whose sources are kept hidden from public knowledge.[164] The lack of transparency undermines the ability to compare the names of funders to the recipient's governing decisions.

Certainly, wealthy businesspeople have tremendous influence over elected officials' decisions. Candidates considered most apt to provide government contracts or influence legislation benefitting them, personally or business-wise, are backed financially. Enormous sums of money are donated to political action committees to bolster candidate campaigns. The concept of "one person, one vote" is skewed when "ad buys" can determine political outcomes.

At the office, employees are urged to support candidates aligned with business prospects. As Mitt Romney told a group of corporate executives during his presidential run, "I hope you make it very clear to your employees what you believe is in the best interest of your enterprise and therefore their job and their future in the upcoming elections."[165]

Politicians are keenly aware of the value of promoting a pro-business platform, given the perceived impact on employment and the general financial health and well-being of the populace. But what pro-business really means is pro–*existing* businesses—assisting the industries and companies that make the biggest campaign contributions.

A real pro-business platform should incentivize creative people to establish new businesses that tackle societal challenges like climate change, equitable employment opportunities, and ethical governance. But because no money changes hands, these noble aspirations fall by the wayside.

A pro-jobs politician can simultaneously accomplish two objectives by sponsoring legislation that supports jobs in clean, sustainable industries, but the politicization of the topic curtails momentum.

Massive numbers of people will lose their jobs, the public is informed, if dying industries that harm the planet and the future of humanity are not given a financial lifeline. That argument may have worked two decades ago, but it is a guarantee of oblivion today.

In fact, the country is immersed in a war for talent, a historic imbalance between companies desperately trying to fill job slots and few people wanting to fill them. This "Great Resignation" came about during the pandemic when many people, worried about their health, financial security, and the new remote ways of working, quit their current jobs to hunt for employment elsewhere. Resignation rates soared among mid-career employees between the ages of thirty and forty-five, who deeply questioned the purpose of the work they performed and the meaning of their lives.

Now is a good time for employers to take their workers' LifeWork contemplations to heart by retraining managers to be more compassionate and empathetic, finding ways to make work less manually burdensome, and deepening their commitments to DEI&B initiatives and their environmental goals. Otherwise, they will lose the war for talent.

Government also needs to direct capital away from bygone industries toward programs that retrain people to work in emerging and sustainable industries. Certainly, a government "of and for the people" should not support any business operation that causes environmental harm, particularly when such support is a quid pro quo for campaign contributions.

Our government will never be equitable, efficient, or effective until the system permitting "bought" elections is dismantled. The

United States should adopt election spending limits similar to those in place in Canada and Great Britain. Televised campaign advertisements should be abolished and replaced with a searchable nonpartisan website comparing candidate positions and past legislative decisions on an apples-to-apples basis. If a successful candidate holds lucrative employer-provided stock or stock options, they should not be allowed to access these funds until after leaving office. Most importantly, they should not be allowed to become a lobbyist after their public service, given how the promise of a future personal relationship with an industry can shape legislation or influence government contracting.

Government career professionals should be respected and fairly compensated for the work they do for all of us. Federal, state, and local governments must commit to providing quality education and healthcare to all citizens. Laws must be consistently enforced in a fair and just manner to keep businesses from behaving in predatory ways. When economic crises cause mass unemployment and small business bankruptcies, as was the case most recently with the COVID-19 pandemic, elected officials must immediately pass legislation assisting financially vulnerable citizens. Providing a safety net for people who fall on hard times is government "of and for the people."

Politicians' character traits must be a consideration in their ability to govern. A history of blatant lies, half-truths, and misleading statements is a clear indicator of a willingness to change the truth to assist personal and business gain. Yes, I'm referring to former President Donald Trump, whose more than 30,500 false or misleading claims during his administration were just the lead-up to the "Big Lie" that the election was stolen, a lie that ignited thousands of his supporters on January 6, 2021, to attack the US Capitol in a failed effort to overturn his defeat in the 2020 presidential election. As horrific as January 6 was, just as frightening is the fact that many politicians later downplayed the incident as a minor disturbance, even after expressing their outrage immediately following the event.[166]

PUBLIC POLICYMAKING FOR
ALL PRIVATE CITIZENS

In addition to focusing on the needs of people today, the government also must take a central position in redressing past injustices. Nevertheless, it cannot do it alone. Given the many industries that profited from slavery, US businesses must collaborate with the federal government to make up for past sins.

Many such businesses are well-known companies like the insurance giants Aetna and New York Life, which sold life insurance policies on the lives of slaves to their owners. Banks like J.P. Morgan accepted slaves as collateral and payment for loans. Railroads used slave labor to build part of their rail lines. The financial center of the world, Wall Street in New York City, was the site of one of the country's largest slave markets. In fact, slaves helped build the wall from which Wall Street derived its name. Georgetown students voted to tax themselves to pay descendants of enslaved people who are responsible for the very existence of the school.[167]

The time has come for companies and institutions that directly and indirectly profited from slavery to partner with the federal government in a comprehensive plan of reparations to change the story of race in our country forever. The reputational currency alone derived from these actions will provide a return on the investment in the form of customers and talented people eager to work for these organizations.

Reparations is not a nice thing to do—it's the payment on a promissory note. It's money that's owed, and it's been collecting interest. Other countries have owned up to these debts, but not the United States. Reparations are compensation to groups of people for historical crimes and wrongdoings committed against them. Germany, South Africa, Colombia, and Kuwait are among the nations that have drafted policies to transform others' suffering into redress. These reimbursements are not limited to money, although that's the most common compensatory form.[168]

After the horrific murder of George Floyd, the subject of reparations is again in the crosshairs of legislative possibilities. A few weeks after his death, the California Assembly established a task force to develop proposals for reparations. At the federal level, Rep. Sheila Jackson Lee (D-Texas) announced in February 2021 the reintroduction of H.R. 40, a bill to create a reparations commission studying the role the federal and state governments played in supporting slavery, as well as the continuing racial discrimination against the descendants of enslaved Africans. The Judiciary Committee of the House of Representatives voted on April 14, 2021, to move H.R. 40, the Commission to Study and Develop Reparation Proposals for African-Americans Act, to the House floor for full consideration after being introduced at every congressional session since 1989.[169]

Anyone with half a mind and half a heart already knows Black Americans have endured centuries of untold hardship and discrimination. That's a given. What is more difficult to discern is what needs to be done in response. For one thing, it is mathematically impossible for Black Americans to catch up to the 400-year head start enjoyed by non-Black Americans. Moreover, giving cash payments to every Black person would be problematic. As we have learned with lottery winners, some people would use the money wisely; others would not.

Reparations should not be a once-and-done payment. Rather, a more comprehensive approach is needed. This approach would require businesses and the government to work together to develop the following:

1) An Equity Account for all Black citizens.
2) A national training course on diversity, equity, inclusion, and belonging.
3) Free college or career training.
4) A national entrepreneurship program for Black citizens.
5) Free access to a trained staff of mental health professionals.

Equity Account

Reparations equal to the net-present value of 40 acres would equate to about $80,000 for each descendant of slaves.[170] That is a good start. To put this number in context, Japanese Americans were paid $20,000 each ($1.6 billion in the aggregate, in 2021 dollars) for their three-year internment by the US federal government during World War II. Slavery, on the other hand, persisted for 245 years.[171] A more accurate reparations figure would include: wages lost during slavery, the economic impact of being shut out of the labor market post-slavery, the destruction of successful Black towns like the aforementioned Greenwood neighborhood in Tulsa, Oklahoma, in the 1920s, the effect of redlining and housing discrimination post–World War II, and the systemic discrimination Black people still face across various aspects of life in America.

Economists can calculate a figure that takes all of these harms into account in devising a fair and equitable plan. The money would be deposited into an account and managed much like a 401(k) plan, where it can earn interest. There should be limited withdrawal options, such as to pay qualifying existing debt or purchase a home. Minors should have Equity Accounts established for them. All the options would be designed to reduce or eliminate debt and build wealth.

National Training Course on Diversity, Equity, Inclusion, and Belonging

Diversity training is another step toward resolving past injustices. Regrettably, many programs are unproductive at best and destructive at worst. Trainers often fail to explore the historical systems and structures causing today's job, income, and other disparities. Moreover, the approach has been more "kumbaya" than science, leading to a lack of credibility. There isn't even a common language and agreed-upon framework for diversity training. This is unnecessary with so many credible sources of available information. The backlash in the early 2020s against teaching about the atrocities committed against people based on race is devastatingly misdirected. We must understand our history to understand its lingering impact. This can be achieved through effective DEI&B training.

Another problem with diversity training is access. Not all companies offer these programs. Rarely is training provided in K–12 schools. And although churches comprise some of the most segregated communities in America, diversity is a subject rarely broached.

To be effective, a government-funded national diversity training program must adhere to the following guidelines:

1) The training must be free and accessible to people virtually, as well as through in-person meetings at various locations in communities.

2) Emotional intelligence should be at the heart of the training, so people can not only understand the challenges but put that knowledge into action.

3) The training must be based on science and taught from an interdisciplinary perspective, rather than anecdotal and siloed.

4) Aside from passion, trainers must also possess a keen understanding of human behavior.

5) The training must stress that White, straight, cisgender, Christian, non-disabled, wealthy, patriotic males are not the

problem. Racism, homophobia, genderism, religious bias, ableism, classism, xenophobia, and sexism are the problems. Rather than feeling anger, despair, or guilt, people need to walk away feeling enlightened and empowered.

6) Special effort has to be made to encourage people who would generally balk at diversity training to take classes. A tax rebate or other financial incentive to people who complete the training can serve this purpose.

Even with the suggested guidelines in place, the training will fail if it is delivered on a one-size-fits-all basis. Rather, it should be provided at a pace customized to people's readiness levels. I have developed the Culture Knowledge/Activity Matrix to serve as a framework to understand where people are on these issues.

Cultural Knowledge/Activity Matrix

	Misinformed	Uninformed	Informed
Progressively Proactive	Re-Educate	Educate	Reinforce
Progressively Reactive	Re-Educate	Educate	Reinforce
Inactive	Re-Educate and Inspire	Educate and Inspire	Inspire and Support
Regressively Reactive	De-Radicalize and Re-Educate	Educate	Redirect
Regressively Proactive	De-Radicalize, Re-Educate, and Re-Direct	Educate and Re-Direct	Redirect

Information Level

Informed people understand the opportunities and challenges associated with DEI&B in America. They are knowledgeable about the country's history regarding these issues and understand the legacy and continuing impact of that history.

Uninformed individuals are not educated about issues of DEI&B. Some of them are actively uninterested in these issues; others just don't have to deal with them in their lives.

Misinformed people are prone to believe information from unreliable sources. These individuals latch on to conspiracy theories and information designed to manipulate them into believing deceptive sources. They tune in to cable news programs, radio talk shows, and social media sources that present biased information masquerading as facts. This is a potentially dangerous group of people; as they become entrenched in their beliefs, they may be influenced to commit violence. It can be extremely difficult to move people from this category because of the "backfire effect"—when presented with facts that counter their beliefs, they may dig their heels in deeper.

Activity Level

Progressively Proactive believe that all people are created equal and should have equal opportunities to achieve personal and professional success. They are activists on the front lines. People in this category are vocal and spend a great deal of effort trying to convince people of the merits of their cause, despite the risk of personal harm. They attend rallies and are active on social media.

Progressively Reactive people are not the type of people who get engaged in these issues until something significant occurs to prompt action. The George Floyd incident is a perfect example. Once the attention on the issue erodes, they become less engaged.

Inactive people may hold a certain ideological perspective yet are restrained to act on their beliefs. They might perceive the issue as too big to tackle or are just too focused on the challenges of daily life to spend much time on issues like race.

Regressively Reactive people may be just as passionate about maintaining the status quo or stepping backward regarding social issues, but they are less likely to act on those feelings until a major incident occurs, such as the insurrection on the nation's capital.

Regressively Proactive people believe some groups are genetically superior. The White Nationalists threat is seated in this group. Just like Progressively Proactive people, they are activists on the front lines but on the other side. They are active on social media, constantly trying to recruit new followers.

The most despicable among these categories are Informed, Regressively Proactive individuals (the bottom right corner of the model). This group has been instrumental in creating and perpetuating America's tragic disparities through their neuro-manipulation of working-class White people. Members of Congress, for instance, have access to the most accurate information about issues of racial bias and discrimination. Experts testify before them and present findings from all the latest studies, yet they ignore this data to curry favor from their often uninformed or misinformed constituents.

The appropriate interventions in the matrix include:

- De-radicalization, which is required for people who express hateful, extremist sentiment.
- Education, which provides the knowledge and information individuals need to make more informed decisions.
- Redirection, which is required for people who are actively working against diversity, equity, inclusion, and belonging (DEI&B).
- Inspiring and supporting people who have been disengaged.
- Reevaluating the monopolization power of social media giants like Facebook, following whistleblower revelations that the company puts profits ahead of its members' mental health and well-being.

INTERCULTURAL SENSITIVITY

Diversity training also needs to take into account intercultural sensitivity. One model that captures this concept is Milton Bennett's "Developmental Model of Intercultural Sensitivity."[172] This intuitive framework is a continuum that begins with several "monocultural mindset" stages, before moving on to various "intercultural mindset" stages. Bennett defines "monocultural" as consciously or subconsciously using one's own set of cultural practices to judge all people. Intercultural, on the other hand, is more of the "when in Rome, do as the Romans do" mindset.

The early monocultural stages of Bennett's model address conscious behaviors that are negative, mean-spirited, and outright discriminatory. The model subsequently explores subconscious microaggressions, the small transgressions people commit unintentionally, followed by what Bennett calls "minimization." In this stage, people believe the problem is talking about our differences and the solution is to focus on our similarities instead. The primary criticism of this perspective, which led to the concept of America as a "melting pot," is the pressure it imposes on minority groups to assimilate into the dominant culture, as opposed to integrating their unique experiences into what should be an evolving culture.

The intercultural stages of the model involve the recognition, acceptance, and appreciation of our differences. Eye-opening life experiences that challenge uninformed and narrow perspectives should be sought out, not avoided or minimized. Perhaps attend a service at a Black Baptist church and a Bahai Temple—not to compare which is "better" but to learn more about others' belief structures and where they are different from, similar to, or overlap with one's own beliefs.

Delving into another culture's distinctiveness may appear intimidating at first, but don't let that stand in the way of the need to challenge preconceived notions of cultural differences. Achieving this goal requires proactive, intentional effort to acquire information about different cultures, such as watching foreign movies and documentaries and reading novels from authors in distant lands. Travel to different countries or venture into American cities and neighborhoods with large groups of a particular culture. Try learning a new language or spend time with a mentor or mentee from a different cultural background.

Free College or Career Training

Higher education is a necessary but not sufficient aspect of closing the gaps between White and Black people. It bothers me when I hear people say, "Well, college is not for everyone." The statement can be paralyzing for children without a family history of going to college. It also gives many kids an excuse not to dream big. People say things like, "I did not go to college, and I turned out okay." They make comments like, "My uncle worked as a carpenter and now owns his own business; he never went to college." They say, "Billy never went to college, and he is a millionaire now." These outcomes do happen, but they are not the norm and are hardly relevant in the aggregate.

For me personally, college was more than an opportunity to prepare for a job or career; it represented the possibility of changing my life. At the University of Illinois, I learned to find an apartment, pay bills, buy groceries, vote, and make healthcare decisions. I learned how to be a self-starter, as my class attendance and performance was entirely up to me. I also learned that diversity was about more than just Black and White. This is the case for many White students who experience living and working with non-White people for the first time.

My life was enriched by the quality and variety of people I met at the university. A college campus is designed with learning as its centerpiece. Scholars, writers, artists, and political figures were common visitors. My time away at school prepared me to negotiate the challenges and complexities of life. Money should not be a barrier to this kind of experience.

The movement toward free college education for students at certain income levels has gained steam in recent years. At least fifteen states cover the cost of tuition for some students to attend traditional four-year colleges and two-year community colleges. Nearly forty communities have made college tuition-free through so-called Promise Programs. According to the Campaign for Free College Tuition, funds for the programs are provided by a combination of private philanthropy and community commitments.[173] Other funding is provided by agencies using the Community Link Foundation's procurement model, social impact bonds offered by private investment funds, and local employers who support associate degree programs generating the skilled workers they need. If the federal and state governments spent taxes funding public school education more judiciously, enough money would be on hand to fund every child's education at a public college.

The free college tuition movement for low-income individuals is promising for Black kids who grew up in communities like the one I came from, as well as for White kids who also grow up in difficult circumstances. But the issue is bigger than income. Many middle-income and even high-income Black people also need access to such programs. Not only do these individuals experience bias and discrimination, but they lack the level of savings and net worth as their White peers with similar educations and incomes. They do not live in the same communities, enjoy the same lifestyles, or have the financial capability to send their kids to the same colleges, despite incomes that would suggest otherwise. White people have inherited money and assets passed down from ancestors who were not limited by Jim Crow sanctions, which has compounded over the decades.

A National Entrepreneurship Program

Vulnerable and stressed, Black people simply want to give their kids resources and opportunities they did not have. An untapped opportunity to achieve wealth for Black people is the ownership of a successful business. A major marketing campaign aimed at inspiring young Black people to become entrepreneurs should be launched. For the new ventures they create to have the best chance of success, the need for initial resources must be taken into consideration. One way to meet such needs it through the creation of a national endowment to provide startup capital to promising Black-owned businesses across the country.

Some companies are interested in the value of launching their own programs. The Lowe's program with *Shark Tank* star Daymond John mentioned in Chapter 5 is one example. They invite Black and other underrepresented entrepreneurs to apply for a chance to pitch their products to Lowe's executives and win some shelf space in their stores.[174]

Other ideas on the development of entrepreneurship programs include:

1) Businesses can provide capital to sponsor a statewide entrepreneurship contest in predominately Black high schools.

2) Rather than just fund the development of Black-owned barber shops and hair salons for Black people, lenders' emphasis should be placed on establishing businesses that attract more diverse clientele. Asian people and other groups open businesses that provide products and services for customers of any background. Examples include health and wellness clinics, health food stores, health-focused restaurants, and fitness centers. These options are viable given that Americans of all backgrounds struggle with obesity and associated chronic health issues, particularly those living in poor communities.

3) A matchmaker program can be established to link people with great ideas to those with the skills to turn ideas into business ventures. An individual with a great idea for an app, for example, could be paired with a programmer who could design it.

4) Capital should be made available only to people who complete required training courses and consistently meet with a business mentor. This training would be similar to a crash-course MBA, designed to give new business leaders the skills and experiences they need to become successful. Courses should be offered in person and/ or online.

5) Robust entrepreneur programs need to be established at historically Black colleges and universities. The programs could pair students with professors to establish a start-up business that is beta tested at the university. During the

summer, the program can provide internship opportunities at existing start-ups.

6) Special effort should be made to engage rehabilitated convicts and current inmates, as many have demonstrated the same skills running their illegitimate businesses that are required to run legitimate businesses.

Mental Health
Counseling and Support

More than one-quarter of all adults suffers from a diagnosable mental disorder in a given year.[175] Imagine the percentage of Black people that persistently experience racial discrimination and the long-term psychological, emotional, and physical disorders caused by this trauma. Yet most Black people do not receive treatment for the lingering stigma caused by racial discrimination. Those that consider mental health counseling often are hesitant to talk to White therapists about their experiences, and there are few Black therapists.

A way around this divide is to create a cultural competence program preparing White mental health professionals to better understand the Black experience in America. A nationwide recruitment effort also should be undertaken to recruit talented Black students interested in mental health careers. Financial and other support should be offered to these students to overcome barriers impeding their education and the establishment of a mental health practice.

Whether White or Black, mental health professionals can improve positive thinking and discourage negative thinking, enhancing learning and optimism. Black people recruited to go into this field will encourage other Black people to receive the help they need, with the added benefit of improving educational attainment and increasing employment levels in a community.

To attain these goals, mental health professionals should be trained to help patients become more resilient. In *Resilience: The Science of Mastering Life's Greatest Challenges*, authors Steven Southwick, MD, and Dennis Charney, MD, point out the need for people to have adequate social support and access to resilient role models, possess cognitive and emotional flexibility, have meaning and purpose in their lives, and engage in both physical fitness and what the authors call "brain fitness."[176]

White people also would benefit from a clearer understanding of what it means to be Black in America. Hate and guilt are mental health problems that require treatment. Many White people, for instance, are torn between family loyalties and personal convictions on the subject of race. I met such an individual years ago, following a speech I gave on race relations. Almost in tears, the young White woman said her parents had exposed her to a constant stream of hate-filled speech and other negative conditioning about race. Both parents were active members of an extremist group, wore their attire at group meetings, and spewed invective on which race was "naturally" superior and "naturally" inferior. She wanted her children to grow up with a different perspective, but she didn't know where to start.

She was brave to challenge her parents. But she clearly struggled with how people she loved could hate others based simply on the color of their skin. I listened to her with understanding and empathy, but I am not a professional mental health counselor. I advised her to contact someone who was. If more people in her position did the same thing, the impact of racism on them and on the long-term psychological, emotional, and physical traumas to Black people will diminish.

A WORLD-CHANGING INVESTMENT

The debate in America about government versus business is misdirected. We need business *and* government to work together to solve the problems facing our country. High on the list of priorities is making amends for America's original sin. This is not a question of funding, but rather a question of priority and public will. America spends about $50 billion per year on foreign aid.[177] As responsible global citizens, it is important that we continue to contribute to countries in need. But we cannot turn away from the experiences and needs of Black citizens at home. By temporarily diverting some of the capital earmarked for foreign aid into partnerships with businesses promoting Black entrepreneurship, education, mental health counseling, and so on, amends can be made.

The good news is that Corporate America is finally recognizing its responsibility to a subset of stakeholders: Black employees and customers. Their ancestors fueled the growth and development of many US industries and large corporations. It is time for government and business to level the playing field for all Americans, giving everyone a shot at long-term success.

Reparations are amends for wrongs one has done, in this case slavery and its equally vile antecedents. It is about countless lives snuffed out or squandered. It is about the relentless infliction of physical pain and suffering and mental anguish. But it is also about settling an unpaid debt for the hundreds of millions of hours of free labor Black people provided in lifting America to become a global economic powerhouse. It's time for government and business, in partnership, to even the score.

For this to happen insists upon a widespread acceptance of truthful narrative. America's history of racism has existed from the days of slavery, through the creation of the United States, through decades of Jim Crow laws, through one Reconstruction after another to change the status quo. Is it possible to celebrate the brilliance of our nation's founders in their conception of a place where the Constitution's First Amendment provides five guaranteed freedoms to the people of the United States of America, making them the freest in the world, yet criticize the fact that Black people were not included in this pledge? Can their good deeds be appreciated despite their woeful shortcomings? The answer is yes, as human beings, by our nature, are imperfect.

Terrible mistakes were made through the centuries, resulting in truly horrific crimes against Indigenous people, Black people, and every wave of poverty-stricken immigrants seeking the promise of the American Dream. Reckoning with these crimes against humanity requires their full telling, as uncomfortable as that may be for some people. Sugar-coating them in school classrooms and textbooks to preserve the illusion of unblemished American greatness will impede the transformation of our country into the singular place the founders had the wisdom, courage, and grace to create in the first place. Our search for humanity depends upon our will to accept the truths of our checkered history—to learn from them in building a new tomorrow.

[156] "Federal Government Contracting for Fiscal Year 2018 (Infographic)," WatchBlog, May 28, 2019, https://blog.gao.gov/2019/05/28/federal-government-contracting-for-fiscal-year-2018-infographic/.

[157] Daniel E. Slotnik, "Edwin Kosik, Firm Judge in 'Kids for Cash' Case, Dies at 94," *The New York Times,* June 14, 2019, https://www.nytimes.com/2019/06/14/us/edwin-kosik-firm-judge-in-kids-for-cash-case-dies-at-94.html.

[158] Kara Gotsch and Vinay Basti, "Capitalizing on Mass Incarceration: US Growth in Private Prisons," The Sentencing Project, August 2, 2018, https://www.sentencingproject.org/publications/capitalizing-on-mass-incarceration-u-s-growth-in-private-prisons/.

[159] Louis Jacobson, "Chris Matthews Says Cheney Got $34 Million Payday from Halliburton," PolitiFact, May 24, 2010, https://www.politifact.com/factchecks/2010/may/24/chris-matthews/chris-matthews-says-cheney-got-34-million-payday-h/.

[160] Matt Egan, "Trump Adviser Gary Cohn's $285 Million Goldman Sachs Exit Raises Eyebrows," CNNMoney, January 27, 2017, https://money.cnn.com/2017/01/26/investing/gary-cohn-goldman-sachs-exit-trump/.

[161] Luqman Adeniyi, "Steve Mnuchin Received Nearly $11 Million in Severance from CIT Group," *CNBC,* March 30, 2017, https://www.cnbc.com/2017/03/30/steve-mnuchin-received-nearly-11-million-in-severance-from-cit-group.html.

[162] Maggie Koerth, "How Money Affects Elections," FiveThirtyEight, September 10, 2018, https://fivethirtyeight.com/features/money-and-elections-a-complicated-love-story/.

[163] Ciara Torres-Spelliscy, "20 Things We Learned About Money in Politics in 2020," Brennan Center for Justice, December 8, 2020, https://www.brennancenter.org/our-work/analysis-opinion/20-things-we-learned-about-money-politics-2020.

[164] "Presidential General Election Ad Spending Tops $1.5 Billion," Wesleyan Media Project, October 29, 2020, https://mediaproject.wesleyan.edu/releases-102920/.

[165] David A. Graham, "Can Your Boss Threaten to Fire You If You Don't Vote for Romney?" *The Atlantic,* October 20, 2012, https://www.theatlantic.com/politics/archive/2012/10/can-your-boss-threaten-to-fire-you-if-you-dont-vote-for-romney/263709/#.

[166] Cristina Marcos and Rebecca Kheel, "GOP Downplays January 6 Violence: Like a "Normal Tourist Visit," *The Hill,* May 12, 2021, https://thehill.com/homenews/house/553227-gop-downplays-jan-6-violence-like-a-normal-tourist-visit.

[167] Saahil Desai, "Why Are Georgetown Students Paying Reparations?" *The Atlantic*, April 18, 2019, https://www.theatlantic.com/education/archive/2019/04/why-are-georgetown-students-paying-reparations/587443/.

[168] Kim Hjelmgaard, "Reparations Bill Gets New Attention Amid BLM. Could Other Nations Provide a Blueprint?" *USA Today*, July 10, 2020, https://eu.usatoday.com/story/news/world/2020/07/10/slavery-reparations-bill-spurs-new-debate-other-nations-model/5396340002/.

[169] "Historic Progress on US Slavery Reparations Bill," Human Rights Watch, April 15, 2021, https://www.hrw.org/news/2021/04/15/historic-progress-us-slavery-reparations-bill#.

[170] George Pierpoint, "The US Students Who Want to Pay Slavery Descendants," BBC News, April 10, 2019, https://www.bbc.com/news/world-us-canada-47886292.

[171] Isabella Rosario, "The Unlikely Story Behind Japanese Americans' Campaign for Reparations," NPR, March 24, 2020, https://choice.npr.org/index.html?origin=https://www.npr.org/sections/codeswitch/2020/03/24/820181127/the-unlikely-story-behind-japanese-americans-campaign-for-reparations/.

[172] Milton J. Bennett, "The Developmental Model of Intercultural Sensitivity," IDRInstitute, 2014, https://www.idrinstitute.org/dmis/.

[173] "Who We Are," The Campaign for Free College Tuition, accessed January 25, 2022, https://www.freecollegenow.org/who-we-are.

[174] Jeanne Sahadi, "This Shark Tank Star is Partnering with Lowe's to Help Minority-Owned Businesses," CNN., September 16, 2020, https://edition.cnn.com/2020/09/15/success/lowes-daymond-john-minority-entrepreneurs/index.html.

[175] "Mental Health Disorder Statistics," Johns Hopkins Medicine, accessed January 25, 2022, https://www.hopkinsmedicine.org/health/wellness-and-prevention/mental-health-disorder-statistics.

[176] Steven M. Southwick and Dennis S. Charney, "Resilience: The Science of Mastering Life's Greatest Challenges," Cambridge University Press, August, 2012, https://www.cambridge.org/core/books/resilience/767FAF256DEFE3EF6B122FE4500FA189.

[177] Kieran McConville, "Foreign Aid by Country: Who's Getting the Most—and How Much?" Concern Worldwide US, October 7, 2021, https://www.concernusa.org/story/foreign-aid-by-country/.

CONCLUSION

In Search of a Solution

Americans are as polarized as we have ever been in our lifetimes. Politicians take crude shots at each other with no regard for peoples' lives. Family members are estranged. People avoid coworkers and neighbors, and strangers engage in violence against each other. At the heart of it all is race, a made-up concept originally used to justify human bondage and generate precisely the kinds of divisions we are experiencing today. We cannot decide if our future must be that of a progressive nation that values all its citizens or one that prolongs the caste system by assigning outcomes based on race.

The past was extraordinarily traumatic. Black people were brought to America as slave labor in 1619. For nearly 250 years, slaves were the foundation of America's economic prowess. They endured unthinkable mental and physical trauma, including family

separations, sexual assaults, breeding, castrations, beatings, and murder. Even after they were emancipated in 1835, it was still legal to discriminate against Black people until 1965. Since then, Black people have continued to experience bias and illegal discrimination in all aspects of life, *throughout their lives.*
The present is extraordinarily painful. Black people still suffer a disproportionally high rate of infant mortality. They still attend segregated, inadequately funded schools. They are paid less than their White peers at every level of education. They suffer a higher rate of unemployment at every level of education. They have a higher response rate to their job applications when they remove any evidence of being Black. They are offered less when selling their homes and charged more in interest when buying new homes. They are arrested at a higher rate, convicted more consistently, and receive harsher sentences than White people who participate in the same behaviors. When unarmed, they are killed by police at significantly higher rates than unarmed White people. They are more likely to be victims of hate crimes than any other group. They are treated unequally by the healthcare system, suffer disproportionally higher rates of chronic health conditions, and experience a lower life expectancy rate than anyone else in America.

Many White people, despite ample evidence that includes booming membership in hate groups, either deny this rampant inequality or accept no complicity—Black people are merely playing the "race card" and using excuses for their own lack of effort. When Black people complain about unjust treatment, they are often told, "If you don't like it, leave," as if they are here as unwelcome houseguests.

Some White people protest that they are under assault from having to listen to Black people's continual griping.

If it is frustrating to hear about these issues, imagine how taxing it must be to live them and watch family members and friends live them as well. If you are White and agree with transparent evidence on systemic racism in America, it is your responsibility to call out the White people dividing the country. They make life hard for everybody.

The future can be extraordinarily fruitful. To comprehend why these injustices still exist and how such formidable obstacles can be overcome, we must understand the role the human brain plays. Our brains have been wired through human survival instincts to make us gather into tribes of similar-looking people. This evolutionary inheritance cannot be overcome without emotional intelligence and critical thinking.

Americans must recognize and value each other's humanity. Nobody chooses their parents or where they are born. We do not determine our lives; chance determines it for us. The fact that kids in communities all over the world experience more significant challenges than our kids is beside the point. None of those countries claim to be what America says it is. America must reckon with its ideals of "life, liberty, and the pursuit of happiness" for *all* of its citizens.

For America to thrive and its citizens to live healthier, happier lives, we must turn the very thing that has caused us so much turmoil—our diversity—into the very thing that makes us special. Race, religion, sex, gender, sexual orientation, age, and socioeconomic status are all important elements of the rich tapestry that strengthens and binds us. Our differences should not separate us or be ignored; rather, they must be cherished. We are all Americans. I am not a Black American, but an American who is Black.

To generate pride and reverence among all Americans, our government and society must make amends. Black people never received the promised "forty acres and a mule" for the blood, sweat, tears, and countless lives of generations of slaves extinguished in the establishment of America's place on the world stage. Treating Black people today as lesser citizens who don't deserve to be here adds to the interest due on this promissory note.

The business community can help change the narrative. Business and government must partner in the development of programs and initiatives that level the playing field and judge people on their own merits. These actions will generate opposition from White citizens who don't want a level playing field. Their vision of America remains tribal. To counteract this backlash, we must come together to say enough is enough, to rise up and realize our nation's tremendous potential.

ACKNOWLEDGMENTS

A lot has changed in my life since I published *The Fragile Mind: How It Has Produced and Unwittingly Perpetuates America's Tragic Disparities* in 2008. Most notably, the birth of my two kids. It has been such an incredible experience seeing the world through their eyes. As I learn more about them, I learn more about myself each day. Thank you, Alex and JC, for being my primary source of pride and inspiration.

Thank you, Adrienne, my wife and best friend for over twenty years. Every idea I have and argument I make in my writing and speaking is strengthened by your pragmatism and attention to detail. Everyone should be lucky enough to have a partner like you.

To my sister, Jessica, it's just you and me now. We have got to take care of each other. I also want to thank my nieces and nephews, Chandria and Jalen, Shelondra and Mikayla, and Ortega, as well as my in-laws and special family members Carlos, Shelby, and Wendell. I hope this book is something you can be proud of because discussions and interactions with you over the years helped shape my perspective.

Thank you to all my colleagues at the various stops along my professional journey, including several impactful internships: McDonnell Douglas (now Boeing), Union Carbide (now Dow), Pillsbury (now General Mills), Dain Rauscher Wessels (now RBC Wealth Management), Citibank, CSX, the Jacksonville Regional Chamber of Commerce, and the City of Jacksonville. I want to thank the leadership at UKG for supporting my efforts and my staff and other colleagues for being great sounding boards and offering meaningful feedback. I also want to thank the many nonprofits that provided me an opportunity to serve on their boards to help make a difference in people's lives.

I am fortunate to have built strong bonds with my brothers of the Greater Beta Chapter of Kappa Alpha Psi and the Archons of Sigma Pi Phi in Jacksonville, Florida, and San Diego, California. These relationships have been a significant source of encouragement, support, and wise counsel. I also have a strong fraternity of brothers from my original hometown of East St. Louis, Illinois. We have supported each other and kept each other grounded for over thirty years. As the years roll by, I gain more appreciation for how lucky I am to have such deep, authentic relationships. Thank you to my editor, Pulitzer-nominated author Russ Banham, for his tireless efforts in helping me get this ready to submit, as well as the entire staff at Scribe who worked on this project.

Finally, I want to thank all the people who have attended presentations and keynotes I have delivered over the years. There have been days when my optimism about the future of humanity wavered, but your wide smiles, approving nods, high level of engagement, and kind feedback have powered me to push forward and remain dedicated to doing all I can to leave a better world for your kids and mine.

HUMAN LIKE ME

We must change what it means to be an American and reinforce what Americans look like—humans of all backgrounds. We must rally around a vision of America that promotes diversity, equity, inclusion, and belonging.

To help generate this kind of momentum, I have created a Human Like Me campaign consisting of apparel that you can purchase to proudly demonstrate your respect and appreciation for all humans.

You can purchase these items at www.humanlikeme.com. A percentage of your purchase will be donated to a charity whose mission it is to eradicate bias, bigotry, and racism.

CPSIA information can be obtained
at www.ICGtesting.com
Printed in the USA
BVHW080158160922
646956BV00001B/35